D0394904

# Our Sisters
in the Bible

# Our Sisters
# in the Bible

Jerrie W. Hurd

Deseret Book Company
Salt Lake City, Utah

ISBN 0-87747-981-x
Library of Congress Catalog Card Number 83-50986

First printing October 1983
Second printing January 1984
Third printing January 1985

*To Jon*

*and my first readers, whose comments were invaluable: Ruth Simmoneau, Judith Toronto, Susan Early, Crystal Heer, and Vicki Heer.*

# Contents

# Preface

Many of my Latter-day Saint sisters believe that women are hardly mentioned in the standard works of the Church. They wonder if that apparent dearth of women in the scriptures implies insignificance. At first glance the scriptures may fail to provide a strong impression of women, but there are reasons for this: individual women are rarely spotlighted; groups of women and anonymous references tend to fade into the background; the topical guide includes few entries dealing with women; and so on.

Actually, the scriptures, especially the Bible, are rich with womanly examples, but to see them, one must focus on them. The terms *wife*, *woman*, and *mother* can be easily skimmed over. Noting them establishes that women took part in events and creates a more balanced picture of family life in ancient times. Too often we see only Moses, when in the same text we could see Shiphrah, Puah, Jochebed, Miriam, and Zipporah. It helps to ask, while reading of battles and migrations, what the women were doing. In some cases, it is necessary to piece the stories together. The story of Sarah is a good example. It is scattered throughout the narrative of Abraham. Because entire chapters are devoted to Abraham's activities and only a few verses to Sarah's, we tend to lose track of her, making her seem shadowy next to her husband. If, on the other hand, we read all the verses about Sarah at one time, she emerges as a strong, spiritual individual who coped well in difficult situations.

Nearly a hundred women are cited by name in the Bible. Several of the same women are also named in the Book of Mormon, Doctrine and Covenants, and Pearl of Great Price. Other women are mentioned in terms of the deeds and roles they performed. In Kings and Chronicles, for example, the phrase, "And his mother was . . ." is often linked with "and he did that which was good (or evil) in the sight of the Lord."

Hebrew women were honored as mothers and wives, but their influence, the dimensions of their lives, was not limited to those roles. Women served as ministers in the temples, as diplomats, midwives, weavers, dancers, innkeepers, harvest gatherers, and more. They ruled nations and households. They started and stopped wars. Some sinned. Others walked uprightly. In every case, however, they made and acted on their own decisions.

The stories of the more famous of these women, Esther, Ruth, Hannah, and so forth, are at once both familiar and ever fresh. Why, one wonders, do they live so vividly in the imagination? Is it because they happen to have been enshrined in scripture? Or is it because they're so palpably alive?

*Our Sisters in the Bible* recreates these women as real human beings struggling with problems not unlike those women face today. It attempts to understand and interpret their spiritual experience, their faith, and their relationship with God. In a larger sense, it suggests that all women are sisters—the beloved daughters of the same Father.

# 1
# *Eve*

Woman, as well as man, is God's crowning creation. Eve was the last of the six days' work God called "good." Like Adam, she was fashioned in God's image. With Adam, she was given charge over all the earth. (See Abraham 4:27-31.)

In the second chapter of Genesis, God states that human- kind is not complete without both sexes. "It was not good"—it was not perfection—for the man to be without the woman, or the woman without the man. Neither could achieve exaltation, the ultimate purpose of creation, without the other. Sex is not an afterthought, nor is marriage a civil contract. Marriage means becoming coequal with creation; it is a sacrament in which the laws of morality and the laws of nature are integrated. Adam understood this principle. When he saw his bride for the first time, he burst into poetry: "This is now bone of my bones . . . flesh of my flesh: she shall be called Woman."

By the third chapter of Genesis, Eve steps forward as a woman of independent will and individual responsibility. The tempter came, and as tempters do, he suggested some niggling motive behind God's restrictions. Eve answered him with a shattering innocence: "We may eat of the fruit of the trees of the garden: but of the fruit of the tree which is in the midst of the garden, God hath said, Ye shall not eat of it, neither shall ye touch it, lest ye die."

With half-truths, the tempter painted the downward path as leading up. He said, "Ye shall not surely die: for God doth know that in the day ye eat thereof, then your eyes shall be opened, and ye shall be as gods, knowing good and evil."

The account goes on to say that the woman saw that the tree was good for food, that it was pleasant to the eye and something to be desired to make one wise. Eve's temptation was threefold: physical (good food), sensual (delightful to the eye), and spiritual (promised wisdom). The sophistication with which Satan laid his scheme reveals how he perceived our mother, Eve. Satan didn't see her as inquisitive, weak, deceitful, or ambitious. He didn't insult her intelligence. If anything, he appealed to her sense of adventure.

Eve has often been maligned for her transgression. A convenient peg upon which to hang unflattering theories about women, she has been blamed for bringing death and sin and work into the world. Fortunately, revelations restored in this dispensation correct that view. As a Latter-day Saint, I know that Eve in no way frustrated the plans of God. Rather, I owe her respect for her courage, which ultimately allowed me, her daughter, to be born. In the Book of Mormon, Nephi writes, "After Adam and Eve had partaken . . . they were driven out of the garden. . . . Adam fell that men might be." (2 Nephi 2:19, 25.)

Likewise, the Genesis account does not separate the man from the woman. Though Adam did not pluck the fruit, he willingly partook. When God confronted him with his transgression, he said, "The woman whom thou gavest to be with me, she gave me of the tree, and I did eat."

Also confronted by a questioning God, Eve explained, "The serpent beguiled me, and I did eat."

Those answers can be read as honest statements of what happened as readily as attempts to place blame. Neither Adam nor Eve justified their sin. As one, they knowingly ate; as one, they then faced their punishment.

Yet they would never again be as totally "one" as while they were in the garden. In Eden, "they were both naked, the man and his wife, and were not ashamed." But immediately after sinning, they became uneasy with each other; "and they knew that they were naked; and they sewed fig leaves together, and made themselves aprons." Somehow their sin had disrupted the most fundamental relationship in the world, that between man and woman. If recrimination was intended in the statement "She gave me of the tree, and I did eat," it was doubtless the mutual recrimination of the sexes, born of sin and a new tension that had come into the world.

Other punishments were also natural consequences. When God said to Eve, "I will greatly multiply thy sorrow and thy conception," he described conditions resulting from her transgression. Yet Eve's was a pleasing punishment. Her desire for her husband was to be as great as his desire for her. Despite the pain and travail of childbearing, she was to be preserved and would know maternal joy. She was to be called the "mother of all living."

The couple's work was to be the bearing, supporting, teaching, and rearing of children. Knowing this, God did not leave them alone to face their new challenge. In Moses we read that "they heard the voice of the Lord from the way toward the Garden of Eden, speaking unto them, and they saw him not; for they were shut out from his presence. And he gave unto them commandments. . . . And Adam knew Eve his wife, and she conceived and bare Cain, and said: I have gotten a man from the Lord."

Eve knew that her child came not merely from her flesh,

but from God. By the time her first child was born, God, not the serpent, ruled her life, for she had risen above her transgression. She already knew of the Redeemer and looked forward to his coming.

I am sure it was to the birth of the Redeemer that Paul alluded when he spoke of Eve and her daughters, saying, "Notwithstanding she shall be saved in childbearing." It is not the physical act of bearing children that saves womankind; it is the Savior, born of a woman through Eve's lineage, who saves.

Yet no matter how perfectly Eve understood the plan of salvation, she was handicapped as all mothers are. She could not force her knowledge upon her son, nor could she love that knowledge into him. With the birth of Cain came the first generation gap, for he did not know the experiences of his parents. To him, the garden was only a story. We read that "Cain hearkened not, saying: Who is the Lord that I should know him?" (Moses 5:16.)

Eve suffered the anxieties, heartaches, and torments suffered by all mothers of disobedient children through the centuries. We are told that "Adam and his wife mourned before the Lord, because of Cain." (Moses 5:27.)

But Eve, evidencing some of the same courage with which she ate the fruit, did not give up hope: "And Adam knew his wife again; and she bare a son, and called his name Seth: For God, said she, hath appointed me another seed instead of Abel, whom Cain slew." (Genesis 4:25.)

"And God revealed himself unto Seth, and he rebelled not." (Moses 6:3.)

Eve's creation is described with the same wonder as the stars, the sun, the moon, and all the other things God created and called "good." From the rapture with which Adam greeted her, I assume that she was pleasing to look at—not in the sense of high fashion, but in the sense of radiant, healthy vibrancy. The serpent approached her with great subtlety and respect. She fell, but in doing so she furthered God's plan and made mortality possible. Eve was teachable. When her association with God dwindled to hearing his voice somewhere near the garden, she still listened and heeded. Expressing her joy in mortality with great eloquence, she declared, "Were it not for our transgression we never should have . . . known good and evil, and the joy of our redemption, and the eternal life which God giveth unto all the obedient." And then, we are told, "Eve blessed the name of God, and they [Adam and Eve] made all things known unto their sons and their daughters." (Moses 5:11-12.)

I am proud to be one of those daughters. I am moved to know that my mother, Eve, wanted her offspring to have the same joy she experienced. Though she was frustrated, disappointed, robbed of one son, and shamed by another, through it all she persevered. Eve was the first woman, the first wife, the first mother, and the first repentant sinner. Adam called her the "mother of all living," but Eve earned her name.

Scripture references: Genesis 1, 2, 3, 4; 5:1-2; 2 Corinthians 11:3; 1 Timothy 2:13; 1 Nephi 5:11; 2 Nephi 2:18-25; Mosiah 16:3; Alma 12:21, 26; 42:2, 7; Helaman 6:26; Ether 8:25; Moses 2:27; 3:21-25; 4:6-27; 5:1-27; 6:2,9; Abraham 4:27-31; 5:14-21; Doctrine and Covenants 20:18-20; 138:39

# 2

# *Sarah and Hagar*

A t first I thought Sarah was lost in the shadow of her husband. Although extolled by many (including the apostle Peter) as a model, obedient wife, she is too quickly passed over. Under closer examination, however, I began to view her not as submissive, but as quietly confident. She felt a true affection for her husband Abram, a feeling he returned in kind. Never in any of their wanderings, trials, or disappointments, did he presume to interfere with her authority—not even when it concerned the bondwoman Hagar and the son he had fathered by her.

Hagar was Sarah's sorest trial in a life that seemed a continuous testing of her faith in God's promises. But Hagar, too, was tried. When circumstances and her own haughtiness brought her to the point where she had no reason to expect special consideration, God befriended her and gave her a promise. It was not Sarah's promise, but her own, and it was more glorious than any she might have hoped for.

Similarly, God overwhelmed Sarah. After she had despaired, given up, scoffed at the thought of being blessed, she suddenly found herself the fulfillment of all that had been covenanted. Such bespeaks the closeness, the individuality of God's relationships with his female children.

She was called Sarai when, in her mid-years, she left her settled home in the teeming, cultured city of Ur and took up the life of a nomad. In the company of her husband Abram, their father Terah, and their nephew Lot, she traveled to Haran, the place of their family origins. There Terah died. There too, after Abram saw the three daughters of Onitah sacrificed for refusing to relinquish their beliefs, and after nearly becoming an offering himself, he received his first call from God: "Get thee out of thy country, and from thy kindred, and from thy father's house, unto a land that I will shew thee. And I will make of thee a great nation."

Once again leaving their home, Sarai and Abram traveled through the wastelands. When Lot became disagreeable, Abram separated from him. Sarai shared her husband's purpose and his dreams, and she was willing to share the heartaches and trials that went with them.

In the plain of Moreh in the valley of Shichem, Abram built an altar. He later built altars on a mountain east of Beth-el and on the plain at Mamre. Sarai worshipped with him at these altars, becoming, as Peter says, "heir" with Abram of "the grace of life."

Then a famine drove them to seek refuge in Egypt. Women of Sarai's day considered travel the one thing most fatal to beauty; yet when Sarai arrived in Egypt, her still-radiant beauty was enough to cause a minor sensation. It was a matter of course in those days for a prince to help himself to any handsome woman who caught his eye, and to kill her husband if the husband objected. Knowing that Sarai's beauty would endanger Abram, the Lord suggested that he conceal his real relationship to her. (See Abraham 2:22-25.)

Being so directed, Sarai agreed to call herself Abram's sister. It was a partial truth, as Sarai was indeed Abram's half-sister. They shared the same father.

As they feared, Pharaoh immediately took Sarai into his harem, giving Abram substantial presents of sheep, oxen, camels, and servants. From that moment, however, things went badly for Pharaoh. A series of plagues came upon his court. The historian Josephus credits Sarai herself with the negotiations that won her release. Courageous and faithful to her marriage vows, she admitted to her royal admirer that she was the wife of Abram and the cause of the present difficulties. Fearing divine displeasure, the Pharaoh called for Abram, giving him more presents, and sent Sarai away with him.

I can only guess at what that experience meant to Sarai. She had been inside the harem in the palace of Pharaoh. Even the briefest stay in that center of power among the beautiful women gathered from Greece, Phoenicia, Arabia, and Ethiopia must have been an education.

In the events to follow — the separation of Abram and his nephew, the battle of the kings, the imprisonment and rescue of Lot, and the receiving of the blessing of Melchizedek — the scriptures make no mention of Sarai except to suggest that during her husband's absence she took charge, assisted by his steward.

The magnitude of her responsibility is best expressed in numbers. At Abram's call, no less than three hundred eighteen servants, born in his house and trained to arms, accompanied him to rescue his nephew. Assuming that those left behind to tend Abram's numerous flocks and herds must have been at least equal in number, the complete entourage could have consisted of some six hundred forty able-bodied men, not including women and children. Over these people Abram exercised absolute power. He delegated that authority to Sarai in his absence.

Even when her husband was at home, Sarai shouldered considerable responsibility. She directed the women who produced many of the essential goods for the family. These women ground meal, baked bread, wove cloth, and made clothing. They carried water, gathered herbs, and entertained guests. They were the guardians of medical and hygienic information, caring for the sick as well as bearing and rearing the children. This they did as members of a camp that was always on the move.

I interpret the silence of the scriptures as evidence of Sarai's competence. She executed her responsibilities without complaint or reason to be complained of. She might even have prided herself on her position and on the promise God had made her husband, if it had not been for her growing fear, as the years passed, that she was the obstacle to its fulfillment.

Concubines were common during this time, and I find it remarkable that neither Sarai nor Abram had resorted to such means of having children before they did. It was ten years after they left Haran before Abram took Hagar to wife—ten years since he had first received the promise. There is no indication that he ever reproached Sarai for her barrenness, though as the years passed, the flocks and herds increased, but Abram didn't.

Because in the scriptures years of history are condensed into a few words, it sometimes seems that biblical characters lived charmed lives. This brevity can lead to the misconception that favored servants of God were spared day-to-day frustrations, that they were immune to crushed hopes and human emotions. Nothing could be further from the truth. Yet only once did Abram betray his grief. In secret, he chided the Lord, saying that he from whom a great nation was to spring had only a servant for an heir. The Lord responded with a reiteration of his promise.

Acting under the "law of Sarah" (see D&C 132:65), Sarai suggested that Abram accept Hagar as his concubine. They hoped that in his doing so, the promise might be fulfilled. Hagar was an Egyptian, given to Sarai by Pharaoh and taken by Abram and Sarai out of Egypt to a foreign land and a strange way of life. Likely she was young, a favorite of her mistress, and likely she had no say in the matter. She was considered property and was so subservient that the thought of her consorting with Abram gave Sarai the least possible pang. Her child, if she had one, was to be raised by Sarai as her own. The arrangement was an expedient, physical adjustment, with Hagar providing a fertile womb, nothing more.

But when the slave girl conceived, the relationship changed. Sarai was somehow made to assume full blame for the childless marriage. Abram, no matter how perfunctory his embraces had been, could hardly help seeing Hagar as the instrument by whom the promise was to be fulfilled. And Hagar, about to become the mother of her master's heir, could hardly be blamed for taking advantage of her new status. She who had had nothing now possessed the one thing her mistress most desired.

Sarai might have turned her anger inward, but she possessed too great a sense of her own dignity, too full a knowledge of her rights. She was outraged by Hagar's unexpected trammeling of the favor she had herself extended.

In giving herself airs, Hagar underestimated her mistress. Sarai, fully knowing what a child meant to her husband, knowing she had failed to provide that child, and knowing that she herself had suggested that Abram take Hagar, rose up in righteous indignation. She who had been humiliated enough by her barrenness was not about to suffer the sneering triumph of this younger woman.

Abram had been promised posterity. His wife was barren. He had begotten a child upon her bondwoman so that the promise appeared to be within his grasp. Yet when Sarai complained that Hagar had become insolent, he unhesitatingly restored her to her rightful place. He said to Sarai, "Behold, thy maid is in thy hand, do to her as it pleaseth thee."

Sarai dealt harshly with Hagar. She may have physically

abused her. But whatever the punishment, it was not severe enough to cause bodily harm. Hagar still had the ability to flee, and she did. Growing heavy with her master's child, she must have expected Abram to protect and support her. But he hadn't; nothing had changed. Doubly burdened with that shattering revelation, she fled alone into the desert.

If that wasn't sufficient to dash her dreams, in the desert she was addressed by an angel as "Hagar, Sarai's maid." She was told to return and submit to her mistress. In the eyes of God, nothing had changed either. But the angel continued, assuring her that though her master and mistress had put her into this predicament, she and the child she carried were the objects of God's love. She was told that her seed would be multiplied and that her son would bear a name that would ever remind her that God had seen her affliction. She was given other promises as well. When the angel finished, Hagar exclaimed, "Thou God seest me." She then returned to Sarai and Abram and submitted herself to them.

Thirteen years passed, during which Hagar's son Ishmael was reared and treated as Abram's heir. Sarai's last hope of having a child waned and died, but there seems to have been no further enmity between Sarai and Hagar. Sarai may even have formed an attachment for Hagar's child; certainly Abram did.

Then one day the Lord instructed Abram to change his name to Abraham and his wife to change her name to Sarah, preparatory to taking on the long-promised blessing and covenant, marking his descendants as the chosen of the Lord, the lineage of the Messiah, the everlasting inheritors of Canaan. Abraham greeted the announcement with wonder and joyous laughter for Sarah's sake. Yet his affection for Hagar's child made him cry out, "O that Ishmael might live before thee!" The Lord soothed the anxious father with a repetition of the promise he had given Hagar. Sarah's would be the covenant seed; but Ishmael, too, would be blessed and multiplied.

Sarah's reaction to the bestowal of her new name and

this reiteration of the old promise is not described. She probably dismissed it as too painful a recollection of the old hopes she had already laid to rest. But shortly after the announcement, Abraham offered his hospitality to three strangers. They foretold the destruction of Sodom and Gomorrah and the birth of Isaac. Listening at the tent door, Sarah laughed to herself. Having a child at her age seemed as likely as fire coming out of heaven to consume the wicked cities on the plain.

She was immediately chastised. God asked Abraham, "Wherefore did Sarah laugh? . . . Is anything too mighty for the Lord?" Her innermost thoughts revealed, she tried to deny that she had laughed, but was silenced. Yet there was a certain meekness about the rebuke, calling her not so much to repentance as to greater faith. The promise flashed back as brightly and vividly as when it was first given, and Sarah must have known in an instant that all the years she had waited, all the bitter humiliations she had suffered, had not been in vain.

A strange incident follows. Before the birth of Isaac, Abraham took his camp into Gerar, where Abimelech was king. By this time Sarah was ninety years old, yet her beauty became a problem once again. Abraham resorting to his earlier stratagem, introduced her as his sister. Again she was immediately drawn into the king's harem; again God troubled the king, and again Sarah was restored to Abraham with gifts and the king's pledge of free passage across the land. I wonder if, in regaining her ability to conceive, Sarah was somehow rejuvenated, her beauty and youth restored. However it came to pass, Sarah conceived and gave birth to a son. She named him Isaac, meaning, "laughter."

Hagar's son was immediately deposed. Despite his seniority and the years of privilege he had enjoyed, he was still a slave's child, always to be ranked beneath a son of Sarah, be it the first or the tenth. To Hagar, the birth of Isaac must have been a grievous disappointment, and to the young Ishmael, educated with the idea that he was his father's heir, the change in his status must have seemed cruel and confusing. This state of affairs continued three, perhaps four years, until Isaac's weaning festival, during which Sarah noticed Ishmael mocking her son. With lightning prescience she saw the dangers of keeping Hagar and Ishmael in her household.

Abraham was less decisive. If Sarah had asked him to punish the pair, no doubt he would have done so. Banishing them was another matter. The scriptures say that "the thing was very grievous to Abraham's sight," and that he sought counsel from the Lord.

The thought of Hagar and her son, expelled from their home and driven into the desert with nothing more than a bottle of water, can easily excite more sympathy than the harsh Sarah, who, for what seems a trifling offense, demanded such severe retribution. Abraham himself must have seen error and misunderstanding on both sides. But the Lord confirmed Sarah's request. Offering Abraham consolation in the promise that he would protect and preserve Ishmael and make him also a mighty nation, the father of twelve princes, the Lord commanded Abraham to listen to his wife.

I feel a touching sympathy for the way Abraham sacrificed his own feelings and let his elder son go. He had flocks, herds, servants, and great wealth, but he gave none to Ishmael. The Lord had promised to provide for the boy; what could he add to that? Taking bread and a bottle of water and placing it on Hagar's shoulder, he sent the two into the desert.

Hagar wandered until the water was gone. Then, not wanting to see her child die, she left him under a bush and went away to weep. She was a slave, praised by none and loved by few except God, who comforted her whenever she asked. He sent her angels and wonderful promises. I can think of few women who could claim to be better blessed than Hagar.

An angel appeared saying, "What aileth thee, Hagar?

fear not." Repeating the promise that Ishmael would become a great nation, God opened Hagar's eyes; she saw a life-giving well of water, and she and her son drank.

The scriptures add that God was with Ishmael as he grew and dwelt in the wilderness. Ishmael became an archer, and Hagar found him a wife among her own people.

The fact that the Lord watches over, protects, and has purposes for all nations of the earth is confirmed repeatedly by the prophets: "Are ye not as children of the Ethiopians unto me, O children of Israel? saith the Lord. Have not I brought up Israel out of the land of Egypt? and the Philistines from Caphtar, and the Syrians from Kir?" (Amos 9:7.) And again, "I remember one nation like unto another." (2 Nephi 29:7-8.)

As God promised, Ishmael became a great nation. Hundreds of years later the Moslem prophet, Muhammad, praised and acknowledged God for the preservation of his ancestress Hagar.

For Sarah, too, things worked out well. Not only was she honored as the mother of God's chosen nation, but she was given the time and pleasure of raising her child free from jealous discord. In that, God was kind. I wonder if the scriptures' silence concerning her role in the near sacrifice of Isaac is a kindness, as well. Was that final trial of faith given to Abraham alone?

Sarah must have known that in his devotion to God, Abraham would not withhold even Isaac. Did she know and trust in him as completely as he trusted God? Or was that the final, searing test of her faith—watching them leave, waiting, not knowing the outcome for six days while they traveled to the mountain and back? Whatever her role, Sarah met the test. She is acknowledged by Paul as one of those great in faith.

The near-sacrifice of Isaac is the best known incident in the life of Abraham. It is also the event in which Sarah is least visible. But in the larger scope of their married life, her presence is unmistakable. Though she lived thousands of years ago in a foreign land, I find her wise and meticulous cultivation of her marriage as laudable today as when Peter and Paul spoke her praises.

Husbands and wives who forfeit spiritual aspirations— God's promises—for more expedient pleasures often find themselves, like Hagar, facing the desert alone. The freedom that allows a person to achieve his or her full potential comes from skillfully balancing individual agency and needs against the rights and needs of the union, sacrificing some to nourish the self much more in the rich medium of a warm, supporting family.

In my opinion, it was such marital skill, not groveling submission, that made Sarah the model, obedient wife. It was that skill that earned her a full and equal partnership in the fulfillment of God's promise. Yet one need not achieve Sarah's excellence to have value in God's eyes. Hagar didn't, and she was visited by angels.

Scripture references:
*Sarah*
Genesis 11:29-31; 12:5-20; 16:1-8; 17:15-21; 18:6-15; 20:2-18; 21:1-12; 23:1-20; 24:36; 25:10-12; 49:31; Isaiah 51:2; Romans 4:19; 9:9; Hebrews 11:11; 1 Peter 3:6; 2 Nephi 8:2; Doctrine and Covenants 132:34-37, 65; Abraham 2:2-4, 15-25
*Hagar*
Genesis 16:1-16; 17:20; 21:8-21; 25:12; Galatians 4:24-25
*Daughters of Onitah*
Abraham 1:8, 11-12

## 3

# *Rebekah*

Rebekah is the wife who tricked her blind old husband into blessing her favorite son, Jacob, when the family legacy should have gone to his elder brother, Esau. The rights and wrongs of that affair echo to this day. Some see Rebekah as a scheming, autocratic matriarch. Others excuse her, saying that while her method was deceitful, her motive was pure. I have no intention of taking either side. To me, Rebekah is far too rich a character to categorize.

Her story begins at the death of Sarah. Likely Rebekah never met her mother-in-law. Abraham and Sarah lived in Canaan, a land distant from their own childhood homes. A sense of that distance burst upon Abraham when his wife died: "And Abraham stood up from before his dead, and spake unto the sons of Heth, saying, I am a stranger and a sojourner with you: give me a possession of a buryingplace

with you, that I may bury my dead out of my sight."
(Genesis 23:3-4.)

Shortly after that, with a deepening sense of his own
mortality and his alienation in Canaan, Abraham called for
his eldest servant, probably Eliezer, and made him vow to
see that Isaac did not take a Canaanite woman to wife. The
servant was to journey back to the country of their origin,
find a woman among Abraham's kindred, and then return
with her to Canaan.

Abraham may have been too old or too ill to make the
trip himself, but Isaac's acquiescence in the choice was taken
for granted. The servant made only one objection: what if
the woman didn't want to come?

Abraham assured his servant that the Lord would send
an angel before him. But if the woman would not come, then
he was to be free of his oath.

Eliezer made the long journey to Mesopotamia. No
sooner had he arrived than, echoing his master's trust in the
Lord, he prayed for direction. He was standing by a well
where the daughters of the city came to fill their water jars;
his prayer was that the girl who gave him a drink and
offered to water his thirsty camels would be the one the Lord
had appointed for Isaac. He prayed that in this way, he
would know the Lord's choice.

The scriptures indicate that even before he finished his
supplication, Rebekah appeared. Described as being "very
fair to look upon, a virgin," she went down to the well and
filled her pitcher.

Eliezer ran to meet her and said, "Let me, I pray thee,
drink a little water of thy pitcher."

She said, "Drink, my lord." When he had finished she
spoke again: "I will draw water for thy camels also." She
emptied her pitcher into the trough and ran again to the well
to draw more water.

Eliezer "wondering at her, held his peace." This is not
surprising. Seldom is a prayer answered so promptly with
such point-by-point fulfillment.

When Rebekah finished watering the camels, the servant took a golden ring and two bracelets and gave them to her. He asked whose daughter she was and if there was room in her father's house to lodge him.

She said, "I am the daughter of Bethuel the son of Milcah, which she bare unto Nahor [Abraham's brother]." She added that there was straw and feed and room enough.

Eliezer bowed his head and thanked the Lord.

Rebekah must have worked hard to refresh those ten camels after their long journey, yet she did it without hesitation. When she was presented with expensive gifts from a stranger, she didn't lose her composure; rather, she was deliberate and systematic. She named her parentage and assured him that his unexpected arrival would not embarrass the household.

Rebekah rises from the scriptures as a lively, intelligent, quick-witted young girl with an unfaltering grasp of the events around her. Rebekah's first thought was to give hospitality; this is also true of her family. Eliezer accepted their graciousness for his camels, but he was too full of his mission, too happy of its success, to eat anything. He begged to be allowed to speak before supper. Describing the wealth and condition of his master Abraham, he declared the purpose of his visit. He recounted all that had happened at the well, including his prayer and its immediate answer. Then he asked for Rebekah.

The men of her household were impressed. They said, "The thing proceedeth from the Lord."

There is some question as to whether the household of Abraham's kin believed in the one true God. A generation later, Laban was still a worshipper of images when Jacob came to live with him. Nevertheless, Bethuel and Laban acknowledged Eliezer's faith and admitted piously that "we cannot speak unto thee bad or good. Behold, Rebekah is before thee, take her."

Not a word from Rebekah is recorded. If she was satisfied with what was happening, she had no reason to speak.

The next morning, when they did ask her, she was decisive. Her mother and her brother wished to have her stay with them a few more days, while Eliezer was anxious to go. At an impasse they sent for Rebekah and asked her, "Wilt thou go with this man?"

She answered, "I will go."

Eliezer felt that once the Lord had made his wishes known, there was no time to delay. Rebekah clearly agreed. She left her home as a girl of good family should, the blessings of her relatives ringing in her ears, her nurse and her damsels riding with her.

Days later, in the cool of the evening, Isaac went out to meditate and, lifting his eyes, saw the camel train approaching. At the same time Rebekah turned to the servant and asked, "What man is this that walketh in the field to meet us?" The servant told her it was Isaac. With her graceful, unerring instinct for doing the right thing, she took a veil and covered herself as a bride.

The servant reported to Abraham, no doubt sharing with him the wondrous way the Lord had chosen his son's wife. The scriptures paint a poignant scene of their wedding night: "And Isaac brought her into his mother Sarah's tent, and took Rebekah, and she became his wife; and he loved her: and Isaac was comforted after his mother's death."

Isaac was forty years old; Rebekah was a young girl. Isaac was heir to the blessing of Abraham, while Rebekah had arrived straight from the world of idol-worshippers. In those days, the wife was expected to adopt her husband's way of life. Yet this new religion Rebekah encountered must have seemed strange to her; it had to do with one God, the land of Canaan, and a chosen seed to whom that land had been given.

We read that shortly after the marriage of Isaac and Rebekah, Abraham took a wife. Keturah and Abraham had six sons: Zimran, Jokshan, Medan, Midian, Ishbak, and Shuah. Still, Abraham insisted on giving all he had to Isaac. One by one, he sent the sons of Keturah away from him into the east country, where they started many of the tribes of southern and eastern Palestine.

One of these tribes, the Midianites, would preserve the priesthood when Israel fell in apostasy. Much later, Moses would be ordained by his father-in-law, Jethro, a descendent of Keturah. (D&C 84:6.)

But the purpose of separating Israel and the eastern tribes was not obvious when it happened; Rebekah must have watched those successive expulsions and wondered: Would all but one of her sons be given to the desert? How she must have struggled with that question—and with her new religion, the spirit of which was so elusive and yet so all-important. Rebekah took all that upon herself by marrying the unknown kinsman from Canaan, and we are told nothing of how she resolved it.

The first twenty years of Isaac and Rebekah's marriage was barren. But then Isaac entreated the Lord for his wife, and Rebekah conceived.

But the pregnancy did not go well. Something was amiss and Rebekah knew it. As the two children struggled within her, she cried out, "Why am I thus?" and sought the Lord for an answer. Speaking directly to Rebekah, the Lord said, "Two nations are in thy womb, and two manner of people shall be separated from thy bowels; and the one people shall be stronger than the other people; and the elder shall serve the younger."

Whatever difficulty Rebekah may or may not have had adopting Isaac's God, it is clear that by the time she conceived, she was fully converted and conversant with the Lord. When she prayed, she received a specific, prophetic answer—that "the elder" should "serve the younger."

At this point, the scriptures compress twenty years into almost as many words. We are told that Isaac preferred Esau because he ate "his venison," while Rebekah preferred Jacob. That seems a strange commentary when we remember that Isaac was a rich man—rich enough to be envied by the Philistines. He had no need of meat brought home from the hunt; yet we are told he loved Esau "because he did eat of his venison." Was he a gourmet, then? Hardly. Rebekah fooled him with a savory dish of goat's meat, an unlikely possibility unless Isaac was fairly indifferent to his food.

Whatever the reason, Isaac preferred Esau. Yet we are not led to believe that Rebekah despised her elder son. Quite the contrary; when she learned that he planned to kill Jacob, she cried out, "Why should I be deprived also of you both in one day?"

Likewise there is no hint of deep dissension between Isaac and Rebekah because of their preferences. The scriptures suggest that they were in absolute agreement on one important issue: Esau's Hittite wives. When he was forty years old, Esau married Judith, the daughter of Beeri the Hittite, and Bashemath, the daughter of Elon the Hittite. Both were a grief to Isaac and Rebekah.

Perhaps Isaac's preference was that of the parent for the wayward child, the one that required the most love, long-suffering, and sacrifice. Perhaps the only difference between Isaac and Rebekah was that she, being more decisive, had come to consider Esau spiritually unworthy earlier than her husband. Whatever the case, the scriptures give unqualified verification to her judgment. It is written that "Esau despised his birthright."

One day, being old, nearly blind, and believing that he was dying, Isaac called Esau and asked him to take his bow and quiver, get some venison, and make a savory meat dish. Then he would give Esau his blessing.

Rebekah overheard and called Jacob, who at first objected to the plan she proposed. His brother was a hairy man, and he was a smooth man. He was afraid his father would feel him, know he was a deceiver, and curse him. His mother replied, "Upon me be thy curse, my son: only obey my voice."

Isaac's five senses had to be fooled. God had taken care of his sight, and his sense of taste must not have been acute. Rebekah took some of Esau's clothes, which had his scent, and some hairy goatskins, and dressed Jacob in them, covering his arms and hands. It was Jacob's voice that nearly gave him away. When Isaac called his son near and felt him, he complained that his voice was the voice of Jacob; but he was satisfied that the hands were Esau's. Isaac then blessed Jacob, saying, "God give thee of the dew of heaven, and the fatness of the earth, and plenty of corn and wine: let people serve thee, and nations bow down to thee: be lord over thy brethren, and let thy mother's sons bow down to thee: cursed be every one that curseth thee, and blessed be he that blesseth thee."

Can a blessing be given to the wrong person? Isaac owned wells at Esak and Sitnah and Rehoboth. He had great flocks and fields and followers. He was respected by the Hittites and feared by the Philistines. Yet he had only one blessing of significance—the blessing of his father Abraham. That blessing could be given equally to two or ten or twenty sons. It derived no special virtue from the order of its bestowal, but depended upon a worthy recipient. Isaac knew that; therefore, the blessing he conferred upon Jacob, when he thought he was Esau, was not the blessing of Abraham. There was no mention of Abraham in it, or of the land that had been promised to Abraham's seed, or of a multitude of descendants, or of a Messiah through whom all the nations of the earth would be blessed.

Perhaps because he loved both his sons, Isaac hoped to give Esau the first but lesser blessing and Jacob the second but greater blessing. But Esau would not have perceived the difference, because to him the first was the only blessing. If Isaac had had his way, his kindness might have created a nation of pretenders. The Edomites for generations would have had a basis for claiming they had the birthright of Abraham. I believe that this was what Rebekah sought to circumvent. Decisive by nature, she could not let Isaac bless Esau first, even out of love.

When Isaac learned of the trickery, he "trembled very exceedingly." Yet there is no record of any remonstration, reproach, or curse as Jacob had feared. Isaac was pained, but tolerant. When Esau asked for a blessing it was given, and he was promised that his "dwelling shall be the fatness of the earth, and of the dew of heaven from above." Although Isaac has given Jacob power over his brother in the first blessing, he revoked that statement in Esau's blessing, promising him that he would shake off his brother's yoke. The two blessings are substantially the same. Isaac gave Esau what he had intended all along; it was only Esau, with his limited spiritual understanding, who felt cheated.

Nevertheless, the situation was highly charged with anger and resentment. Esau vowed to wait only until his father was dead before taking revenge on his brother. Rebekah had to do something. She could have had Esau expelled, now that the rightful lineage had been declared. That, after all, was how Abraham had protected his heir. Instead, she gave up her beloved son Jacob.

She went to her husband. He was not angry, and he listened as she complained again about Esau's Hittite wives. She said she would consider her life wasted if Jacob married similarly. Isaac agreed.

He summoned Jacob and commanded him not to marry a Canaanite woman, but to go to Padanaram, to the house of his mother's father, and find a wife there. Then Isaac blessed Jacob a second time, declaring, "And God Almighty bless thee, and make thee fruitful, and multiply thee, that thou mayest be a multitude of people; and give thee the blessing of Abraham, to thee, and to thy seed with thee; that thou mayest inherit the land wherein thou art a stranger, which God gave Abraham."

*This* was the blessing of Abraham. Isaac gave it to Jacob knowingly. And Rebekah sent him back to her own people saying, "Flee thou to Laban my brother . . . and tarry with him a few days."

What Rebekah had hoped would be a short separation stretched out twenty years or more. She may not have been alive when he returned. Isaac greeted Jacob, home from

Padanaram with his two wives, two concubines, many sons, and vast flocks. Esau, too, was reconciled and greeted his brother. Rebekah is not mentioned. We know nothing of her death.

Years later, after Jacob's return, the scriptures add one final note: "Deborah Rebekah's nurse died, and she was buried beneath Beth-el . . . and the name of it was called Allon-bachuth [the oak of weeping]."

How much of Rebekah's character did she owe to her faithful nurse? As little as we know about that and much more, it is hard not to admire Rebekah. She accepted a long journey and an unseen bridegroom. She made a place in Isaac's heart equal to his mother's love. She sought the Lord in prayer and received an answer. When she perceived the need, she seized her younger son's destiny and took bold steps to secure it forever. If that constituted deception, she atoned by sending her son far from her. Such courage begets a deep admiration.

Scripture references:
*Rebekah*
Genesis 22-29; 35:8; 49:31; Romans 9:10
*Keturah*
Genesis 25:1-4; 1 Chronicles 1:32-33
*Esau's Wives*
Genesis 26:34; 28:9; 36:2-30

# 4

# *Leah, Rachel, and Their Handmaids*

No man binds himself for seven years and then, when he finds he has been cheated, labors another seven, unless he's madly in love. The fact that Rachel hardly deserved such devotion is only one of the many ironies in the strange mix of the heavenly and the earthly, the spiritual and the sensual woven through the history of Jacob and his wives.

The main characters form a dynamic trio. Leah, the vulnerable, unattractive victim of a lifelong frustration, clung desperately to the man she loved. Rachel, the beautiful, the charmed, felt life owed her happiness and became petulant when it didn't fulfill her expectations. Jacob, gentle and affectionate, became rich despite every obstacle placed in his way. Theirs is a tale complete with passion and unrequited love, a story complicated by their own jealousies and duplicities, a narrative that might be only entertainingly sentimental if not for the fact that Leah, Rachel, and their handmaids gave birth to the twelve tribes of Israel, forming a vital link in the lineage of the Savior. Petty as their motivations seem on the surface, their lives served a divine purpose.

Jacob traveled five hundred miles from Palestine to Padanaram. This was the same journey Eliezer had made to find Isaac's bride. But Eliezer had come with servants and camels and gifts; Jacob came with only his father's blessing, a dream of ladders and angels, and the Lord's promise to be with him. He had nothing to offer a bride but himself and the sweat of his labors.

Stopping at a well covered by a great stone, where three flocks of sheep were waiting to be watered, Jacob asked the shepherds if they knew Laban, his mother's brother. They pointed to Rachel, who was approaching with a flock of sheep, and said she was his daughter. Immediately Jacob rolled the stone from the well, watered her sheep, kissed her (a respectful salutation), and wept. Undoubtedly he had heard the story of how Eliezer had discovered Rebekah at a well, and because he was close to his mother in his heart and far from her in distance, he must have felt that Rachel was destined to be his wife. It was love at first sight.

Rachel ran to tell her father. He greeted Jacob and invited him to his home. A month later, they struck the marriage bargain. Laban was shrewd, hard, devoid of generosity. Jacob, too, drove a hard bargain and was not above being unscrupulous when it suited his purposes. Running through this love story is a subplot of the two men's craftiness; each of them seeming to have met his match in the other. Laban had two daughters. The older, Leah, was "tender eyed" or weak eyed; the younger, Rachel, was "beautiful and well favoured." Laban and Jacob agreed on seven years' service for the younger daughter.

Jacob's fulfillment of that contract stands as one of the unsurpassed expressions of romantic love to be found in the whole of literature: ". . . and they [the seven years] seemed unto him but a few days, for the love he had to her."

At last the wedding feast was celebrated. As was the custom, the bride was conducted to the bedchamber of her husband in silence and darkness. Not until morning did Jacob discover he had been deceived; Leah, not Rachel, lay at his side.

Rachel's reaction to the deception is not recorded. The victim of her father's selfishness (he not wanting an unmarried daughter to support), she was shunted aside, losing the position of Jacob's first, birthright wife. Never would she be the undivided head of her husband's household, but she would be obliged to share all with her older sister.

Fuming little, Jacob accepted the situation. He must have recognized the irony. Leah, led by her father's deceit, had stolen her sister's blessing—as Jacob, led by his mother, had stolen his brother's. And his wrath may have been mitigated by the fact that his veiled bride did not stand in the way of his heart's desire.

It was Leah who gambled the most. She loved Jacob. There is no indication that Rachel loved him more or even as much. Yet Leah must have known that the day after her wedding, the greatest of all humiliations might await her. Jacob might loathe her. Yet she took the risk to have him for one night. Hoping to prove herself the woman for him, she lay in the darkness embracing him.

The morning of her humiliation dawned, and Jacob struck a new bargain. Leah's father snatched one concession: she was to have a week's unrivaled attention from her husband. But the love that couldn't be won in a night could not be won in a week, and seven days later a second wedding was celebrated. The scriptures state unequivocally that Jacob loved Rachel more.

In the years that followed, a lively competition grew up between the two sisters, but no quarrel is recorded. Rachel never flaunted her triumph as Hagar flaunted hers before

Sarah. She may have been in the habit of pitying her older, less attractive sister, and she may have continued with that superior attitude until Leah began to have children.

Leah conceived and gave birth to Reuben, saying, "Surely the Lord hath looked upon my affliction; now therefore my husband will love me." She then conceived and gave birth to Simeon, reasoning that "Because the Lord hath heard that I was hated, he hath therefore given me this son." When she gave birth to Levi, her hope was that "this time will my husband be joined unto me, because I have born him three sons." Upon the birth of her fourth son, Judah, she said, "Now I will praise the Lord."

Each of her sons raised Leah's status in her home and community. The piety with which she named her sons testifies to her faith in Jacob's one invisible God. Not only did she love the man, but she loved his God as well. Her genuine understanding of the true gospel surpasses any disadvantage she may have felt her new religion would give her. She must have had some vague religious notions before Jacob came, and no doubt she was a diligent student of that gospel after he arrived. Her reliance on the Lord may explain why Leah came to be the more contented of the two sisters, despite her failure in the contest for Jacob's love.

Leah had only her children, and yet Rachel envied her. The only harsh words that passed between Rachel and Jacob concerned her unhappiness because of her sister. "Give me children, or else I die," she demanded of him, and Jacob retorted that he was not God. He had not the power to give or withhold the fruit of her womb.

So Rachel gave her handmaid, Bilhah, to Jacob, that like Sarah she might have a child vicariously. Bilhah conceived and gave birth to a son. Rachel, naming him as if he were her own child, called him Dan, saying, "God hath judged me, and hath also heard my voice, and hath given me a son." When Bilhah gave birth to a second son, Rachel named him Naphtali, saying, "With great wrestlings have I wrestled with my sister, and I have prevailed."

Not to be outdone, Leah gave her maid, Zilpah, to Jacob. When Zilpah conceived and gave birth to a son, Leah noted with good humor, "A troop cometh," naming him Gad. She named Zilpah's second son Asher, exclaiming, "Happy am I."

When Leah's eldest son, Reuben, was old enough to wander by himself, Rachel still had no children of her own. One day Reuben returned to camp with some mandrakes. The mandrake was believed to aid a barren woman in conception; today it is known to have the effect of relaxing the womb. Rachel, seeing Reuben's treasure, begged her sister for the mandrakes. She promised that if Leah would give them to her, she would allow her to lie with Jacob that night. Implicit in that scene is the fact that Rachel was able to govern her husband's affections at will, and Leah was making do with the crumbs of Jacob's attention. Then Leah spoke her only bitter words in the entire recorded narrative: "Is it a small matter," she asked, "that thou has taken my husband? And wouldest thou take away my son's mandrakes also?"

She was entitled to believe that Jacob was her husband and that Rachel had somehow supplanted her. She was, after all, the first wife. She had given Jacob four sons of her own, and two by her maid. By law and tradition she had fulfilled all that could be required of a good wife, and yet she was unloved. With justifiable rancor, she accepted Rachel's offer, then went into the field to meet Jacob and tell him that she had won him for the night.

The mandrakes didn't work. It was Leah who conceived. She named her fifth son Issachar, saying, "God hath given me my hire." When she conceived again and bore her sixth son, Zebulun, she observed that "God hath endowed me with a good dowry." Finally she had a daughter, and named her Dinah.

Only then did God remember Rachel. She had a son and named him Joseph. Joseph, like his mother, was Jacob's favorite. He doted on the youngster.

During the years in which his sons were arriving, Jacob had been cheating Laban—and Laban, in turn, had been defrauding Jacob. As long as the two of them maintained a shrewd balance, the home life, while not elevated in moral tone, remained amiable; Jacob seems to have been contented counting sheep and cattle rather than remembering his vision of the angels and the promise of his birthright. Then two things happened. The balance tipped toward Jacob, and God, in a dream, called him back to Canaan. But his departure was complicated.

According to law, Laban could still claim Jacob's children and wives. Their escape, if they were to make it, must be carefully planned and orchestrated. Like Adam, Abraham, and all the patriarchs before him, Jacob consulted his wives. United in an absence of deep regard for their father, Leah and Rachel answered, "Whatsoever God hath said unto thee, do." While Laban was away shearing his sheep, they departed. Jacob took his wives, his sons, his daughter, his cattle, and his sheep. Rachel took her father's idols.

As with the mandrakes, Rachel was less willing to trust Jacob's God than to lean on tangible devices. She had hoped to ensure their safe journey by taking her father's images. In fact, she endangered them all.

When Laban returned and found the idols gone, he was furious. Arming his servants, he pursued the fugitives—not because of his daughters, his grandchildren, or his cattle, but because of his gods. He pretended to be offended that Jacob would leave without a farewell. Actually, he feared Jacob's God; in a dream, he had been warned not to speak ill of or to detain his son-in-law. So he complained most at the theft of his idols. Jacob, not knowing of Rachel's deceit, swore that whoever had taken the gods would not live.

Laban searched Jacob's tent, Leah's tent, and Bilhah and Zilpah's tents and found nothing. He then entered Rachel's tent. She had hidden the idols in her camel's trappings. With great effrontery she sat on them and feigned menstrual cramps, insisting that she not be disturbed. Deferring to her,

Laban searched the rest of her tent, and, when he didn't find his gods, had to suffer the righteous indignation of Jacob, who then felt justified.

When the recriminations ended, Laban and Jacob reached a reconciliation. They built a pillar of stones between them. Laban then required a vow of his son-in-law that he must not afflict Leah or Rachel or take other wives. Finally, each man vowed not to pass over the heap of stones but to go their separate ways.

The next morning Laban kissed his grandchildren, blessed his daughters, and returned to his home. What that more amiable parting meant to Leah and Rachel can only be surmised. No woman ever relishes choosing between her husband and her father. To have a father's blessing when she picks up her husband's destiny fills the vacancy in her heart that his absence creates. So it must have been for Leah and Rachel, who were facing a new home in a strange land among people they had never met. And there were dangers yet to be faced.

The first was Esau, whom Jacob still feared. Jacob sent messengers ahead; they returned with the news that his brother was approaching with four hundred men. Jacob sent presents; in case that failed, he divided and arranged his ranks so as to minimize his losses if Esau meant to do battle. He placed Rachel and Joseph at the rear where they would be under his personal care. Leah and her sons were farther up. Zilpah and Bilhah and their sons were most exposed. No one could have missed the significance of that order, Leah most of all.

That night Jacob wrestled with a man. At daybreak he discovered that the man was a messenger of God. "I will not let thee go," Jacob exclaimed, "except thou bless me." God changed Jacob's name to Israel and renewed the promise given through Abraham and Isaac. Jacob would prevail and become mighty.

The next morning, the two brothers met. Jacob bowed seven times and Esau embraced him.

Jacob built an altar in Shechem and ordered his household to give up their idols, for he had seen the face of God and had been reconciled to his brother. Whether his instruction referred to the images Rachel took or to other private gods members of his large household may have treasured is not clear.

They continued on past the cities of Canaan and no one pursued them. At Beth-el, Jacob built another altar and received a second renewal of God's promise.

As they departed, Rachel started labor with her second child. It was a hard labor, but her nurse encouraged her, saying, "Fear not; thou shalt have this son also." Dying, Rachel looked on her son and named him Benoni, meaning "child of my sorrow," a name Jacob later changed to Benjamin. Rachel was buried at Bethlehem.

Rachel had ached for children, saying that she would die without them, and she died giving birth. Jacob had sworn to Laban that whoever had stolen his gods would not live, and his words proved prophetic. Yet even that circumstance failed to mar his romantic illusion of this woman. He went on to rise above counting sheep and cattle, overcoming the schemes of his youth to become a great man, a seer and a patriarch. Yet years later, when Pharaoh asked his age, he gave it as one hundred and thirty years, with the observation that, "few and evil have been the days of my life." He had prosperity, a large family, and a son who was eminent in Egypt; but Rachel's shadow touched all. For her alone he had labored, and he had lost her.

There is no indication that following Rachel's death Jacob transferred his affections to Leah. Quite the opposite was true; he doted on Rachel's sons to the point of creating divisions in the family. On his own deathbed, he recalled burying Rachel with a vivid poignancy that transcended the years. Yet he made Joseph promise to bury him in the tomb of Abraham and Sarah—in the tomb where he had buried Leah. So perhaps, although the flame had never burned hot, his heart had grown fond of her.

What Leah lacked in beauty, she made up in loyalty to

Jacob. She was a good mother to their children. The scriptures state repeatedly that God heard and favored her. Through her son Levi passed the priesthood; through her son Judah came the Messiah. But Bilhah, Rachel's maid, wrested the birthright from Leah's firstborn in a strangely ironic fashion reminiscent of Jacob's history. Reuben, Leah's eldest son, lay with Bilhah, and their sin became known. Therefore the first son's birthright was given to Joseph.

Rachel was no intellect like Rebekah. She was not religious like Sarah. A great many of her recorded remarks are either petty or petulant. Yet despite such vacuity, she retained an absolute hold on her husband. We can only conclude that she must have possessed many endearing charms lost to the text. Perhaps some suggestion of her manners are echoed in the gentle virtues of Joseph, the child born of her and Jacob's great love. To her credit is the fact that her courtship was followed by complete fidelity. She, too, waited seven years for her marriage.

Beauty, more than once, has turned the course of history. But beauty alone doesn't produce the enduring adoration that Rachel inspired. Ten centuries after her death, the prophet Jeremiah spoke of Rachel weeping for her children. He was referring to the Ephraimites going into exile and prophesying the slaughter of the babes at Christ's birth. Seventeen centuries after Rachel's death, Matthew wrote of her weeping, comfortless, in fulfillment of that prophecy. In the book of Ruth, Rachel is honored (with Leah) as one who "did build the house of Israel." What better epitaph?

Scripture references:
*Rachel*
Genesis 29-31; 33:1-7; 35:16-26; 44:20, 27; 46:19-25; 48:7; Ruth 4:11; 1 Samuel 10:2; Jeremiah 31:15; Matthew 2:18; 2 Nephi 3:1
*Leah*
Genesis 29; 30; 31; 33:1-7; 34:1; 35:23-26; 46:15-18; 49:31; Ruth 4:11
*Bilhah*
Genesis 29:29; 30:3-7; 35:22-25; 37:2; 46:25; 1 Chronicles 4:29; 7:13
*Zilpah*
Genesis 29:24; 30:9-10; 35:26; 37:2; 46:18

# 5

# The Women Who
# Aided Moses

Behind every great man, the old saying goes, stand two great women—his wife and his mother. In Moses' case, there were at least five, possibly seven. There were Shiphrah and Puah, the midwives of Pharaoh; Jochebed, his mother; Miriam, his sister; Pharaoh's daughter; Zipporah, his wife; and the Ethiopian woman Moses married later. To these women Moses was indebted for his life, his education, and his final vindication as a prophet. From them he learned the need for a family-centered legal system and the power of nonviolent resistance.

Moses did not arm the Hebrews and fight his way out of Egypt, which was what Pharaoh feared. Instead, he went to Pharaoh and demanded that his people be freed. Then he made things difficult enough so that Pharaoh had no other choice. Pharaoh's midwives had been giving him similar options for years.

The Israelites had "increased until Egypt was filled with them." That description is supported by statistics. Joseph brought seventy of his family down to Egypt; six hundred thousand left in the Exodus. The Israelites had averaged a doubling of their numbers every fifteen years.

Then a king arose over Egypt who no longer remembered Joseph. He observed to his people that the Israelites outnumbered them and that they must "deal wisely with them" or they would continue to multiply and eventually rise up against their captors. "Dealing wisely" meant that the Egyptians worked the Israelites harder. Still the Israelites kept multiplying.

Excessive forced labor having failed, the king of Egypt called in his Hebrew midwives, Shiphrah and Puah, and gave instructions: "When ye do the office of a midwife to the Hebrew women. . . ; if it be a son, ye shall kill him; but if it be a daughter, then she shall live."

The idea was good politics. The Israelites were no longer a free people. They wanted to leave Egypt and could not. Still, they were "too mighty" for the Egyptians, and they were multiplying. The Pharaoh might have let them go before they became involved in a war, but that was not politically expedient. The Israelites were a valuable property. So he sought to reduce their population to female laborers—noncombatants.

How did Shiphrah and Puah respond to this request? They said nothing and they did nothing. We are told that they "feared God, and did not as the king of Egypt commanded them, but saved the men children alive."

Pharaoh must have considered Shiphrah and Puah cowardly, corrupt, or both to have entrusted the execution of his policy to relatives of its victims. Perhaps they had cultivated such a reputation among the Egyptians. But their deceptions could not go unnoticed indefinitely, for new male children among the Hebrews would not be overlooked.

In time, Pharaoh called for the midwives and asked them to account. What could they answer? In my opinion, Shiphrah and Puah gave Pharaoh one of the cheekiest excuses ever offered a baffled government leader by a pair of professional saboteurs. They explained that "the Hebrew women are not as the Egyptian women; for they are lively, and are delivered ere the midwives come in unto them." And Pharaoh believed them! He kept the midwives in their office, and we are told that "God dealt well with the midwives: and the people multiplied."

Pharaoh was forced to take more drastic measures. No longer attempting to disguise his policies, he hired reliable assassins and issued an edict: "Every son that is born ye shall cast into the river, and every daughter ye shall save alive." Until then, the Shiphrahs and Puahs of the Hebrew nation had circumvented the worst of Pharaoh's plans. Now it would take more heroic resistance. Israel's deliverer had been born—and must be spared.

Moses' mother, Jochebed, was the daughter of a Levite and also the wife of a Levite. She was a worthy woman, steeped in the faith. Out of her home would come Miriam, the prophetess; Aaron, the priesthood founder; and Moses, the great lawgiver. But first she had to save the child. Aaron, older, had been saved by the midwives' stalling tactics. Moses, however, came under the death edict.

With a mother's faith that God had appointed some mission for her son, Jochebed hid him three months. She must have known from the start that her task would be ever more difficult. When the increasing age and size of the child rendered his concealment no longer possible, she undertook a more desperate plan.

Out of necessity, Jochebed coupled her faith with careful planning. She made a cradle of plaited reeds and water-proofed it with slime and pitch. Then, with a trembling but trusting spirit, she committed the little boat to the river at precisely the spot where she knew the daughter of Pharaoh bathed. I imagine that she herself dared not guard the basket, lest she draw the attention of cruel eyes. But little Miriam, about seven years old, playing among the tall reeds, could watch without attracting notice.

At her usual hour, Pharaoh's daughter came to the river to wash herself; seeing the ark, she sent her maid to fetch it. Awed at the beauty of the baby, she claimed him.

Miriam, perhaps having rehearsed the words, stepped forward and asked, "Shall I go and call a nurse of the Hebrew women, that she may nurse the child for thee?" The compassionate, gentle character of the tyrant's daughter may have been known to the Hebrews, for surely Jochebed had some hope that her plan would succeed. Pharaoh's daughter said, "Go."

So it was that Jochebed came to care for her own son as a royal ward. But like Shiphrah and Puah, her duty lay in a higher authority. She, too, feared God more than she feared Pharaoh. And she faced a challenge greater than the Pharaoh's edict. Her son, she knew, must not only receive the necessary nourishment from her bosom, but must learn of God, that he might not be lost to the idolatry of the Egyptian court. The scriptures tell less of how Jochebed accomplished that task than of how she made the water-proof cradle, but certainly it was with the same deliberate care.

Of Moses' youth we know nothing except that he "was learned in all the wisdom of the Egyptians." (Acts 7:22.) We also know that by the time he reached manhood, he identified so closely and had such strong feelings of loyalty for his own people that he killed an Egyptian whom he saw beating an Israelite. He did not learn that from Pharaoh's daughter or in the schools at Heliopolis. His mother had succeeded in educating him as a loyal Israelite.

Yet we must give Pharaoh's daughter her due. She could not have looked upon the child as merely a delightful plaything. In saving him, she defied her father's decree. If she had had enemies at court, they would have used that against her. She may even have risked her own life. Time and time again, she must have shielded Moses from envy and hostility. The officers of Pharaoh's court would have had no love for an adopted "royal" Hebrew. Like Jochebed, she seems never to have lost faith in the child. The education she gave him proved provident in shaping the character of Israel's great lawgiver. Later, though Moses refused to be associated with Pharaoh's court or to be called the son of Pharaoh's daughter, he kept the name she gave him: "Moses"—drawn from the water.

After killing the Egyptian, Moses fled Egypt and went to Midian, where he met the seven daughters of Jethro. They were tending their father's sheep and attempted to bring them to the well where Moses had stopped to rest, but other shepherds kept chasing their animals away. Moses defended them. They told their father of the incident, and he offered Moses the hospitality of his home.

Zipporah was the oldest of Jethro's daughters. Her marriage to Moses took place shortly after the incident at the well. Missing is the romantic wooing that accompanied Isaac and Jacob's taking of their wives. The rest of Zipporah's story seems to bear out the fact that she was not the great soulmate and companion that Sarah, Rebekah, or Rachel were to their husbands. She bore Moses two sons, Gershom and Eliezer, but she seems not to have had a sense of his mission.

Forty years later, Moses started the journey back to Egypt. With his wife, his sons, an ass, and a walking stick, he headed out across the desert, a humble man traveling toward his destiny. The narrative is obscure and apparently incomplete, but Moses seems to have been troubled because his wife, a Midianite, had refused to allow the circumcision of their sons—or at least of their younger son. Now Moses, called by God to the leadership of his people, was anguished because he had neglected this sacred duty. They halted at an inn for the night and Moses became seriously ill.

Both he and Zipporah saw the illness as a sign of divine displeasure and became conscience-stricken over the fact that they had profaned God's covenant. Zipporah yielded. Moses was too weak to hold a knife, so she seized a piece of flint and circumcised her son. Taking the severed foreskin and throwing it down before Moses, she cried, "Surely a bloody husband art thou to me."

When Moses regained his health, he went on to Egypt, but he may have sent Zipporah and his sons back to his father-in-law, for she is next mentioned in an incident in the desert, after the Exodus, when Jethro came out to see Moses, bringing his wife and sons to him. Moses received them graciously, and Jethro gave his overburdened son in-law some much-needed advice. Nothing more is said of Zipporah. A strong woman of some temper, her legacy to her sons and her husband does not seem to have been a spiritual one, though her sons and grandsons became great leaders.

Miriam had a stronger influence on Moses. From the time she first appears in scripture as the fearless, self-possessed little girl proposing to the Pharaoh's daughter that she get a wet nurse for the newly-discovered infant, her character is evident. We hear nothing of her while Moses is growing up in Pharaoh's house, though it seems probable that she shared some of the same patronage, for when she reappears in the text, she is well-educated.

We know nothing of her life during the forty years Moses was in Midian. Josephus records that Miriam became the wife of Hur, a man who was later closely associated with Moses. (Exodus 24:14.) That connection would identify her as the grandmother of Belzaleel, the artist who worked on the construction of the Tabernacle. (Exodus 31:2.) Likely she lived a full life, fully involved with her people during their long oppression, for while there is no mention of her during Moses' confrontation with the Pharaoh, she emerges immediately afterward as a leader of accepted stature.

After the Israelites escaped the Egyptians through the Red Sea, Moses led a celebration of thanksgiving. According to the scriptures, "Miriam the prophetess, the sister of

Aaron, took a timbrel [a tambourine] in her hand; and all the women went out after her with timbrels and dances," singing one of the oldest and most splendid national anthems, which begins "Sing ye to the Lord, for he hath triumphed gloriously; the horse and his rider hath he thrown into the sea." (Exodus 15:21.) Miriam may have composed the words. "Prophetess" was sometimes used to indicate "poetess," a woman extolling God through ecstatic song. Whether she wrote the poem or not, that joining of Moses and Miriam in the great celebration was to be indicative of women's stature under the laws of the new Hebrew nation.

Besides unitedly leading the devotions on that festive occasion, Miriam supported her brother throughout the formation of the national code. Acknowledging her contribution, the prophet Micah wrote, "I brought thee up out of the land of Egypt, . . . I sent before thee Moses, Aaron, and Miriam." (Micah 6:4.)

Moses envisioned peaceful communities of landholding families and framed laws to foster that ideal, greatly benefiting the women of that day. Wives were no longer property to be bought or sold, and men could not hold women servants for gratification without assuming the obligations of a husband. The commandment "Honour thy father and thy mother" elevated motherhood, making matriarchs equally honored and obeyed with patriarchs.

Women stood equal before the law in other ways. Most notably, in contrast to Syrian and Mesopotamian laws, the Mosiac code assessed penalties based on the injury without regard to the sex of the injured party. While Moses is best known as the "eye for an eye" lawgiver, on more than one occasion he counseled husbands against actions that might turn their wives' love from them and often gave a sympathetic ear to women who sought judgments from him, as in the case of the daughters of Zelophehad.

When Moses divided the land of Canaan, he gave it to patriarchs within tribes. That caused consternation to the five orphaned daughters of Zelophehad: Mahlah, Noah,

Haglah, Milcah and Tirzah. Their father, a member of the tribe of Manasseh, had died in the wilderness; therefore, they would have no inheritance unless they were allowed claim to their father's portion. They went to Moses pleading their case. Moses asked God, and God declared, "The daughters of Zelophehad speak right: thou shalt surely give them a possession." Moses gave the daughters of Zelophehad land with their brethren and adjusted the law to allow for such circumstances.

Miriam is thought to have had some influence in the framing of Israel's legal system. Israelite women were active in all aspects of their desert life, including the central and most sacred, the construction of the tabernacle. Women spun and dyed cloth for the tabernacle until they had to be restrained, for they had made more than could be used. (See Exodus 35:22, 25-26, 29; 36:6-7.) Significantly, Moses praised the women more for their attitude than their gift, describing them as "willing hearted." On another occasion they surrendered their most prized possessions, their polished brass mirrors, to adorn the tabernacle, and Moses credited them publicly for their sacrifice. (See Exodus 38:8.) Did Miriam lead the women in those activities?

Whatever Miriam's individual accomplishments may have been, two things are clear. First, the Israelites considered her a leader worthy of their greatest honor; and second, she was subject to human failings. As is so often the case, her spiritual fall came in an area that might have seemed the least likely: she spoke against her brother Moses. More than that, she twisted her great talent of leadership into a knot of jealousy and drew her brother Aaron after her.

The specifics are not entirely clear, but the text seems to indicate that Moses married a second time, or that Moses may have married several times (see Doctrine and Covenants 132:38). In either case, Miriam and Aaron objected to this particular marriage on patriotic grounds because Moses took a foreign woman, a dark-skinned

Ethiopian. But the fault Miriam found in the Ethiopian woman was not as grievous as the bitterness rankling in her own soul until she found both the office and the marriage of her brother equally irksome. With Aaron she publicly called the leadership of Moses into question, saying, "Hath the Lord indeed spoken only by Moses? hath he not spoken also by us?"

Miriam and Aaron aspired to joint usurpation of the state power. But the Lord heard them, descended in a pillar of cloud, and stood at the door of the tabernacle. Speaking out of the pillar, God called for Aaron and Miriam and declared: "Hear now my words: If there be a prophet among you, I the Lord will make myself known unto him in a vision, and will speak unto him in a dream. My servant Moses . . . is faithful in all mine house. With him will I speak mouth to mouth."

When the cloud lifted, Miriam was leprous, white as snow. Aaron, seeing her condition, pleaded with Moses on her behalf and Moses entreated the Lord. The Lord commanded that she be shut out of the camp for seven days.

No greater evidence of the high position held by this woman can be found than in the fact that the whole camp of Israel stood still, halted in its march, for seven days while she suffered this terrible rebuke. The scriptures state that "the people journeyed not till Miriam was brought in again."

I wonder about Moses' new wife during that week. Did she feel some pang at the division her marriage had caused between her husband and his family? Did she worry that he might be required to assume the full responsibility of leadership alone? Did she pray for her sister-in-law?

And what did Miriam struggle with? The leprosy? Or did she tremble with the knowledge that her crowning virtues had become her own excesses? Whatever the struggle, her chastisement had good effect. Miriam overcame her haughty spirit, and cleansed of her leprosy, she was forgiven by God and touched by her brother's love. Eschewing the temptation to wield power, she was restored. Aaron remained in his priestly office, and Miriam is subsequently mentioned as a prophetess.

These women who aided Moses are a colorfully mixed lot. Unlike women in legends and folklore of the same period, they appear human and real. They have faults and virtues, they struggle with problems. Overcoming their failings is their greatest achievement. Such realities testify that sacred script contains actual biographies. I can't generate any genuine sympathy for an Aphrodite, or an Isis, but I can comprehend the women who aided Moses. I feel empathy for them and love them as sisters, even though centuries separate us.

Scripture references:
*Shiphrah and Puah*
Exodus 1:15-21
*Jochebed*
Exodus 2:1-11; 6:20; Numbers 26:59; Hebrews 11:23
*Pharaoh's daughter*
Exodus 2:5-10; Acts 7:21; Hebrews 11:24
*Zipporah*
Exodus 2:21-22; 4:24-25; 18:1-6
*Miriam*
Exodus 2:4-8; 15:1-21; Numbers 12:1-15; 20:1; 26:59; Deuteronomy 24:9; 1 Chronicles 6:3; Micah 6:4
*The Ethiopian woman*
Numbers 12:1
*Daughters of Zelophehad*
Numbers 26:33; 27:1; 36:2, 6-11; Joshua 17:3
*Mosiac laws specifically mentioning women*
Exodus 20:10, 12, 17; 21:3-5, 7, 9-10, 15, 17, 20, 22, 26, 28-29, 31; 22:16-18, 22-24; 23:12; Leviticus 10:14; 12 (childbirth laws); 13:29-46; 15:18-33 (menstruation laws); 18:6-23; 19:3, 20, 29; 20:9-21, 27; 21:2-3, 7, 9, 11, 13-14; 22:12-13; 24:10-16; 25:6; 27:1-8; Numbers 5:2-3, 6, 11-31 (jealous husband laws); 6:2-8; 18:11, 19; 30:3-16 (women making vows); 36:6-11 (daughter's property rights); Deuteronomy 3:18-19; 5:14, 16, 21; 7:3; 12:12, 18; 13:6-11; 15:12; 16:11, 14; 17:2-7, 17; 18:10; 20:7; 21:10-21; 22:5, 13-24 (proving virginity), 28-30; 23:17; 24:1-5, 17-22 (widows gleaning fields); 25:5-12 (widow to marry husband's brother); 26:12-15; 27:16, 19-20, 22-23

# 6

# *Deborah and Others Called Prophetesses*

Six women are presented in scripture as prophetesses. In addition to Miriam, the sister of Moses, discussed in the last chapter, Huldah, Anna, Isaiah's wife, Ezekiel's wife, and Deborah are all called by that title. In the cultures surrounding the Israelite nation—the Canaanites, the Egyptians, and the Greeks, for example—certain women were routinely dedicated to the religious vocation. What is unique about biblical prophetesses is that they were all wives and mothers. No vestal virgins removed from the fray of life, these sacred women sprang from the bosoms of their families, citing their domestic accomplishments as one of the credentials fitting them for religious life: "I, Deborah, arose a mother in Israel."

After Miriam, Huldah is the next prophetess named in scripture. Ironically, her time is best described in the Book of

Mormon. (See 1 Nephi 1:4.) Nephi speaks of many prophets prophesying that the great city of Jerusalem would be destroyed. We know from his account that his father Lehi was one; Jeremiah was another. Jeremiah, in turn, names Uriah. But none of these prophets are mentioned in the historical accounts of that day (the books of Kings and Chronicles), with one exception: Huldah.

She was the wife of Shallem; her family were the keepers of the king's wardrobe. In addition to those responsibilities, Huldah regularly received petitioners and gave counsel to those desiring to inquire of Jehovah.

While renovating the temple, the high priest of King Josiah found a manuscript containing religious law. Wondering about its authenticity, he read parts of it to the king. Being disquieted by the message contained in the writings, the king sent both his high priest and his chief scribe to ask Huldah if the manuscript truly contained the word of God. (Note that he did not request that she appear before him, but that he respectfully went to her for advice.)

Questioned as a prophetess, Huldah answered as a prophetess. She attested to the authenticity of the scroll, part of which is found in Deuteronomy, and went on to prophesy, in the name of God, that Jerusalem would be destroyed because the people had forgotten and disobeyed the laws contained in that manuscript. Her personal message to the king was kinder. Because he had humbled himself in the sight of God, he was promised that he would be gathered to his fathers before her prophecy came to pass.

King Josiah was sufficiently impressed to act upon Huldah's message. He had the newly discovered book of law read publicly. He then destroyed the shrines of the heathen gods, reinstated the Levites, and made a personal covenant to keep the commandments. He had been a righteous observer of the ordinances before, but Huldah's prophecy impelled him to assume religious leadership of the nation. Shortly after King Josiah's death, the remainder of her prophecy was fulfilled.

Isaiah's wife and Ezekiel's wife are described as prophetesses, but the title may have been only honorary, distinguishing them as wives of prophets. Nevertheless, each was supportive, even essential to her husband's work.

Isaiah and his wife were not left to decide the names of their children, for God had determined that what he proposed for Israel should ring in their names. They were called "Hasten the Spoil" and "A Remnant Returns." Indeed, what a mother names her children is heard by many ears.

Ezekiel and his wife were particularly close. When she died suddenly, God forbade Ezekiel to mourn. Restraining his tears as a sign to Israel, he set out to warn the people of the coming destruction of Jerusalem, telling them that they would lose their loved ones and be forbidden to mourn by their conquerors.

The title of prophetess continues into the New Testament. In the temple at Jerusalem, Anna proclaimed Mary and Joseph's babe to be the Christ. An aged widow, Anna is described as never departing from the temple but serving God continually day and night. Though the scriptures state precisely her lineage and her age, it is the youthfulness of her spirituality that strikes me most profoundly. Prophets and prophetesses are privileged to know the future, and Anna was young and vital in her hope. She exuberantly confessed the Christ, recommending him to all who sought redemption. Her witness was added to that of Simeon, who had blessed the babe, of the angels who sang at Christ's birth, and of the shepherds who had come to see him.

By all accounts, the best known prophetess is Deborah. She assumed leadership of Israel's military, judicial, and religious institutions at a crucial time and literally saved the young nation from sinking into oblivion. The Israelites, under Joshua, had forced their way into Canaan but had not gained full control of the country, and many years following that initial conquest were marked by skirmishes and an ebbing of national identity. The scriptures point out that because the Israelites were in danger of merging with the surrounding heathen tribes, God allowed the king of Canaan to afflict them, to demand tribute and to scourge them with raids led by his great general Sisera. During this period of oppression, Deborah served as Israel's judge.

It is entirely in keeping with the character of Mosaic institutions that the nation's chief magistrate was a woman. Deborah's appointment is announced in scripture rather matter-of-factly, and she is portrayed as an inspired judge who is well respected. The palm tree in front of her house, where she sits to give counsel, is noted as a national landmark. When she sends for the leader of the armies, he comes, listens, and obeys.

Of her personal life, less is said. It is recorded that she is the wife of Lapidoth, and she identifies herself as a mother. Her accomplishments cover a wide spectrum. In addition to being a wife, a mother, a judge, and a prophetess, she wrote poetry. Her verse ranks today as some of the finest recorded, whether read in the original Hebrew or in translation. From her poetry we know she was gentle, introspective, and intellectual.

When her nation was disheartened, its leadership faltering, Deborah summoned Israel's most capable military leader from his home in Kedesh. She had come to know it was God's will that Israel be set free—not simply that the next battle be won that they might have a few months' respite from their oppressors. The nation was to be truly liberated. She believed it could be done, but it did not occur to her to actually lead the rebellion. Instead, she sent for the most likely man, Barak, and told him that if he would raise an army of ten thousand, she would promise him, as God's mouthpiece, that he would be victorious.

Barak answered, "If thou wilt go with me, then I go; but if thou wilt not go with me, then I will not go." Some interpret that answer to mean that he was afraid. I think not. Rather, I believe that Barak sensed the spiritual insight Deborah possessed and wanted her with him and his army. I think his answer shows him to be a man of supreme moral courage. Without a quibble, he would raise an army; but he knew what he lacked, and he knew that Deborah, a woman, possessed what was needed.

Deborah agreed to go but prophesied that if she went, the honor of the victory would not be Barak's. The Lord would deliver the great general Sisera "into the hand of a woman." Barak likely thought she was referring to herself but respected her enough to accept her prediction.

Envision the army Deborah and Barak faced. According to Josephus, the Canaanites had three hundred thousand foot soldiers, ten thousand horsemen, and three thousand iron chariots. The whole of that army would not be used against an Israelite rebellion, but we know that at least nine hundred chariots were engaged. Against such odds Barak had raised a small army of tribesmen, tired of paying taxes to a distant overlord, led by a woman.

Of the battle itself, the Bible says only that the Lord "discomfited Sisera and all his chariots . . . so that Sisera lighted down off his chariot and fled away on his feet." Josephus describes in more detail how a sudden storm of rain and hail swept down upon Sisera from Mount Tabor, the Israelite's rallying place, and broke over the Canaanite army. The aim of the archers was deflected, and the horses were terrified, breaking free of the iron chariots and running amok among the foot soldiers. All were routed. Deborah's specific role in the battle is not described in either source. Likely she remained at the rear, her army's inspiration, not their swordsman.

That role fell to another woman, Jael. When Sisera was forced to flee on foot, he made straight for a friendly tribe of nomads called the Kenites. They were itinerant metal-smiths who doubtless had a hand in fashioning the Canaanite chariots. A man named Heber was leader of the tribe, but he was not present when Sisera arrived. In his place his wife, Jael, went out to meet Sisera, offered a kind and reassuring welcome, brought him milk and food—"a lordly dish," the scriptures say—and made him a bed. When Sisera asked her to watch at the tent door so that no one would come upon him unawares, she agreed that she would.

Why Jael chose to side with the Israelites is never revealed. Neither is her nationality; she is simply called "the wife of Heber, the Kenite." She may have been an Israelite who had married outside her own race, or she might have been captured in a raid and given to Heber as a prize. She may simply have been tired of the bloodshed, the constant plundering by Sisera and his army. Whatever the reason, it was into her hands, a woman's, as Deborah had prophesied, that Sisera was delivered, and by her hand he died. In those days, everything connected with a tent was a woman's responsibility. Taking the instruments with which she was familiar, a tent peg in one hand and a hammer in the other, she stole toward Sisera. The skull of this great general was probably softer and less resistant than the dry soil where many, many times she had pitched her tent. She deftly pounded the nail through his temples into the ground.

How Jael explained her deed to her husband who had been Sisera's ally is not recounted. Likely having cast her lot with Barak's army, she fled with them. Unquestionably she broke the most honored of all nomadic obligations, the law of hospitality. The Kenites could not have tolerated such an infraction. But for the Israelites, her courage turned a temporary military victory into a stunning success. When Goliath fell, thirty thousand Philistines fell with him. So it was with Sisera's army.

Deborah returned to her home to extol Jael in one of the most beautiful poems ever written. Yet amid all the jubilant nationalism of Deborah's verse is a womanly introspection unknown in any other biblical literature. The woman who wrote those lines could no more have struck a fatal blow with a tent peg than Jael could have penned a sensitive poem. Yet together they had freed Israel.

In her poem, Deborah claims no glory for herself. She calls upon the princes, governors, and people of Israel to join with her in praising Jehovah. Her words describe how he poured down the rain and made the mountains tremble. The translators of the *New English Bible* render her poem as follows:

> For the leaders, the leaders in Israel,
> for the people who answered the call,
> bless ye the Lord.
> Hear me, you kings; princes, give ear;
> I will sing, I will sing to the Lord.
> I will raise a psalm to the Lord the God of Israel.
> O Lord, at thy setting forth from Seir,
> when thou camest marching out of the plains of Edom,
> earth trembled; heaven quaked;
> the clouds streamed down in torrents.
> Mountains shook in fear before the Lord, the lord of Sinai,
> before the Lord, the God of Israel.

Reminding her people of their recent enslavement, Deborah recalls how they were compelled to travel in bypaths because the high roads were crowded with their foes. She then refers to herself as a mother in Israel.

> In the days of Shamgar of Beth-anath,
> in the days of Jael, caravans plied no longer;
> men who had followed the high roads
> went round by devious paths.
> Champions there were none,
> none left in Israel,
> until I, Deborah, arose,
> arose, a mother in Israel.

With freer eloquence, she celebrates the deliverance of Israel, giving praise to patriots and casting arrows of satire on the cowardly. The tribe of Reuben, she asserts, never got around to more than talking.

> They chose new gods,
> they consorted with demons.
> Not a shield, not a lance was to be seen
> in the forty thousand of Israel.
> Be proud at heart, you marshals of Israel;
> you among the people that answered the call,
> bless ye the Lord.

You that ride your tawny she-asses,
that sit on saddle-cloths,
and you that take the road afoot,
 ponder this well.
Hark, the sound of the players striking up
in the places where the women draw water!
It is the victories of the Lord that they commemorate there,
his triumphs as the champion of Israel.
Down to the gates came the Lord's people:
 'Rouse, rouse yourself, Deborah,
 rouse yourself, lead out the host.
 Up, Barak! Take prisoners in plenty,
 son of Abinoam.'
Then down marched the column and its chieftains,
the people of the Lord marched down like warriors.
The men of Ephraim showed a brave front in the vale,
crying, 'With you, Benjamin! Your clansmen are here!'
From Machir down came the marshals,
from Zebulun the bearers of the musterer's staff.
Issachar joined with Deborah in the uprising,
Issachar stood by Barak;
down into the valley they rushed.
But Reuben, he was split into factions,
great were their heart-searchings.
What made you linger by the cattle-pens
to listen to the shrill calling of the shepherds?
Gilead stayed beyond Jordan;
and Dan, why did he tarry by the ships?
Asher lingered by the sea-shore,
by its creeks he stayed.
The people of Zebulun risked their very lives,
so did Naphtali on the heights of the battlefield.

She describes the battle, ending with a solemn prophetic curse.

Kings came, they fought;
then fought the kings of Canaan
at Taanach by the waters of Megiddo;
no plunder of silver did they take.
The stars fought from heaven,
the stars in their courses fought against Sisera.
The Torrent of Kishon swept him away,
the Torrent barred his flight, the Torrent of Kishon;
 march on in might, my soul!

Then hammered the hooves of his horses,
his chargers galloped, galloped away.
A curse on Meroz, said the angel of the Lord;
a curse, a curse on its inhabitants,
because they brought no help to the Lord,
no help to the Lord and the fighting men.

For Jael, she reserves blessings. The outrages committed against wives, mothers, and little children during twenty years of military oppression give energy to her words.

Blest above women be Jael,
the wife of Heber the Kenite;
blest above all women in the tents.
He asked for water: she gave him milk,
she offered him curds in a bowl fit for a chieftain.
She stretched out her hand for the tent-peg,
her right hand to hammer the weary.
With the hammer she struck Sisera, she crushed his head;
she struck and his brains ebbed out.
At her feet he sank down, he fell, he lay;
at her feet he sank down and fell.
Where he sank down, there he fell, done to death.

Then with great tenderness she touches on the mother of the dead general, Sisera, suggesting the grief that might have fallen to the women of Israel except for the nail of Jael.

The mother of Sisera peered through the lattice,
through the window she peered and shrilly cried,
'Why are his chariots so long coming?
Why is the clatter of his chariots so long delayed?'
The wisest of her princesses answered her,
yes, she found her own answer:
'They must be finding spoil, taking their shares,
a wench to each man, two wenches,
booty of dyed stuffs for Sisera,
booty of dyed stuffs,
dyed stuff, and striped, two lengths of striped stuff—
to grace the victor's neck.'

The song ends with a jubilant supplication to Jehovah.

So perish all thine enemies, O Lord;
but let all who love thee be like the sun rising in strength.

When the song ends, so does all scriptural mention of Deborah. The efficacy of Israel's woman judge and prophetess is summarized in a single telling phrase: "The land was at rest for forty years."

But what of the title "prophetess"? In my studies, I have found it to be a term applied variously to wives of prophets, poetesses, and a few women who possessed the power to prophesy, who declared that they spoke God's message, and whose prophecies were fulfilled. Priesthood ordination is not a prerequisite for possessing this gift. Prophecies can be spoken by men and women, adults and children. Moses outlined in detail how a woman could take upon herself the vows of a Nazarite. (See Numbers 6:2-8.) Luke, in the book of Acts, tells of four young girls who prophesied. (See Acts 21:19.) And Jesus, visiting the Nephites, taught their children and opened their mouths. Babes spoke things too wondrous to be recorded. (See 3 Nephi 26:14.) The prophet Joel looked forward to a day when "your sons and your daughters shall prophesy" (Joel 2:28), a promise the angel Moroni repeated to Joseph Smith (see Joseph Smith 2:41). Again speaking to Joseph Smith, the Lord emphasized in his explanation of Malachi that things formerly hidden from the wise would be revealed to babes and sucklings in this dispensation. (See Doctrine and Covenants 128:18.)

Prophecy is more than simply foretelling the future. Prophets and prophetesses are more than mere mouthpieces. When God transmits his word, he endows his messengers with a high degree of independence. Prophets and prophetesses stamp their own personalities and perceptions on the messages they transmit. They are, first and foremost, individuals. The women in this chapter illustrate that concept amply. Miriam was a charismatic leader who supported and counseled her brother. Anna testified of Christ. Deborah received revelation in her leadership responsibilities. Huldah served as a spiritual guide, speaking God's will.

Two other women in scripture are associated with this

title: Noadiah, a false prophetess, and Jezebel, who assumed the title unrighteously.

Prophecy is one of the spiritual gifts all worthy members of the Church have been repeatedly exhorted to seek. (See 1 Corinthians 12:10; 14:39; Doctrine and Covenants 46:22; Omni 1:25; Moroni 10:13.)

> Scripture references:
> *Huldah*
> 2 Kings 22:14-20; 2 Chronicles 34:22-28
> *Anna*
> Luke 2:36-38
> *Isaiah's wife*
> Isaiah 8:3
> *Ezekiel's wife*
> Ezekiel 24:16-18
> *Deborah*
> Judges 4:4-14; 5:1-31
> *Jael*
> Judges 4:17-22; 5:6-24
> *Noadiah, the false prophetess*
> Nehemiah 6:14
> *Four young girls who prophesied*
> Acts 21:9
> *Scriptural poetry written by women*

Miriam's Anthem, Exodus 15:21 (and possibly Song of Moses, Exodus 15:1-19); Deborah's Hymn, Judges 5; Hannah's Song, 1 Samuel 2:2-10; Mary's Magnificat, Luke 1:46-55

# 7

# *Ruth and Naomi*

T he romantic elements of the story come immediately to mind: a young widow marries a wealthy kinsman and lives happily ever after. The tale would indeed be trite, except that the story of Ruth and Naomi centers not on the marriage, but on the sincere affections shared by the two women. While that is a common enough relationship in everyday life, it is one that has been largely ignored in literature—an unfortunate oversight, since the complexities of a woman's character are determined not so much by how or who she marries as by how she comes to view herself and who she chooses as role models. In Ruth's case, the model was her mother-in-law, Naomi.

In a time of economic distress, Naomi and her family were forced to flee their home in Bethlehem and relocate in a foreign land, Moab. The distance between Moab and Israel is not great—a little more than thirty miles. Distance in the scriptures, however, is not always measured from one place to another but by one's state of conversion to one's god. Moab, a nation of idolaters, was, by that standard, a far country.

Naomi and her husband, Elimelech, must have agonized over their decision. They would be faced with the challenge of rearing their sons in a strange place, far from the good influence of friends and family. Surely they considered the possibility that their sons would marry women of Moab. In the end, however, they may have had no choice.

They went to Moab, Naomi's husband died, and her sons did marry Moabite women. Nevertheless, because of Naomi's influence, the family lived together happily for ten years. Likely the Moabite girls, married outside their tribes, looked to Naomi for a steady, reassuring model in circumstances where they felt unsure. Then tragedy struck again: both of Naomi's sons died.

It is to Naomi's credit that at this point she didn't expect anything from her daughters-in-law. She was a practical woman looking at a serious reduction in her prosperity and seems to have had no thought of inspiring further devotion in her daughters-in-law. Acknowledging the hand of the Lord in both the good and the bad, she grieved, not for herself, but because she had nothing more to give them. She determined to go home to her own people and suggested that they return to their own mothers' houses. Her daughters-in-law were young; if they were not burdened with an old woman, they might find husbands again in their own land.

At this point, my heart goes out to Naomi. I can understand how she must have yearned for old friends, for the family she had left behind, for the familiar places of her childhood. Still, I think she made a mistake, the mistake many of us make in times of trouble. She failed to realize how badly her daughters-in-law needed to help her. Naomi, steadfast in the belief that everything depended on her, discouraged them until one turned back. Ruth, however, refused to abandon the older woman.

Ruth is never physically described in scripture. What we know about her are her inner qualities. I admire most her sensitivity. She had enough inner reserves to show Naomi great tenderness, even while she grieved for her own dead husband. She understood Naomi's need to return to her home, and she didn't beg Naomi to remain in Moab. Neither did she insist on caring for her, thereby making her dependent. It was not in her nature to say something like "Oh, well, if you have to go, take this blanket and extra bundle of food and don't forget to write," thereby burdening her mother-in-law with material things and obligations. More importantly, she didn't blame herself for the things she couldn't do, the things beyond her means or ability. Ruth did what she could. She walked beside Naomi.

That was difficult enough, and Naomi hardly made it any easier. Her mind set, she was doggedly stubborn. Even after Ruth declared that she would leave her home, her people, and her gods, Naomi "left speaking unto her." She may have resented Ruth's insistence. After all, now there were two of them—two useless widows seeking hospitality of Naomi's kin. An awkward situation had been made worse.

Naomi had one other fault. She describes herself as coming out of Israel "full," meaning she had a husband and two sons, and going back "empty," suggesting that she counted Ruth as less. Ruth had to have noticed that, but overlooked those faults because of her mighty love for her mother-in-law and the fact that she had embraced the true god.

Ruth may have nominally accepted the God of Israel at her marriage, but her conversion had deepened. When it came time to decide, she cast herself forever on the side of her husband's country, his people, his mother, and his God. Her words have become immortal: "Intreat me not to leave thee, or to return from following after thee: for wither thou goest, I will go; and where thou lodgest, I will lodge: thy people shall be my people, and thy God my God."

Traveling together, Ruth and Naomi journeyed to

Bethlehem. Their thoughts may have been quite different —
Naomi recalling her youth, Ruth noticing the novelty, the
strangeness of the land with a mixture of wonder and appre-
hension. Arriving home, Naomi found many changes.
People that she knew had moved, and the famine that had
driven her family out had taken its toll on others. But some
old friends remained, and they marked the difference in her,
asking, "Is this Naomi?" She answered, "Call me not Naomi,
call me Mara [meaning bitter]."

Poverty-stricken though she was, Naomi did not rush to
her husband's wealthy kinsmen, introduce herself, and
expect to be taken in. There were other ways to provide for
themselves. She and Ruth arrived in the fall while the
harvest was being gathered. Gleaning, according to the
Mosaic law, was the privilege of the poor. (See
Deuteronomy 24:17-22.) Landowners were forbidden to
harvest the corners or to pick up what fell to the ground. But
gleaning was hard work, not suited for an older woman.
Ruth left Naomi and went to the fields by herself.

The people of Bethlehem noticed her. When she came to
her rich kinsman's field, he expressed an interest in her,
saying: "It hath fully been shewed me, all that thou hast
done unto thy mother-in-law since the death of thine
husband: and how thou hast left thy father and thy mother,
and the land of thy nativity, and art come unto a people
which thou knewest not heretofore."

Then secretly he ordered his servants to let more barley
fall, that Ruth might have more to glean. His charity was
offered in a way that would not injure the pride of the two
widows, who had chosen to remain independent. Expecting
no thanks, he hoped Ruth would never know he was helping
her. But Naomi wasn't fooled; when Ruth returned with
more than her usual gleanings, she asked, "Where hast thou
gleaned today?" Ruth explained her encounter with Boaz,
and Naomi expressed her thanks, saying, "Blessed be he of
the Lord, who hath not left off his kindness to the living and
to the dead."

Time passed, and the barley and wheat harvest ended. Everything had been gathered in from the fields and the threshing began. Boaz continued to show more then ordinary interest in Ruth, inviting her to glean only in his field and to share the drink and food of his regular workers. He also took care to protect her from men who might take advantage of her situation. With all that, Naomi finally decided there might be something she could do for her daughter-in-law after all.

Because we know so little about the customs of that day, it is hard to judge whether Naomi's plan was bold or conventional. Unquestionably there was some risk. Boaz was a kinsman, and in ancient Israel, kinsmen had particular responsibilities toward their brothers' widows. (See Deuteronomy 25:5-10.) Naomi knew that. She also knew that Boaz was not her nearest kinsman, but that since he had shown an interest, he might seek to assume that responsibility if he were encouraged. Weighing everything carefully, she decided to instruct Ruth on how a woman could properly approach such a man and seek his protection in marriage.

Relying on Ruth to follow her instructions explicitly, she told her to go to the threshingroom where Boaz would be sleeping to guard his grain from thieves. Washed and dressed in her finest, she was to wait until he was asleep; then she was to uncover his feet and lie down beside him. There was nothing in those actions intended to compromise or entrap him, but merely an attempt to let him know that if he sought to marry the widow of his next of kin, the woman herself would find such an arrangement acceptable.

Ruth obeyed. Boaz was at first surprised, then delighted. He acknowledged both his obligation and Naomi's hand in the affair. Taking care for Ruth's reputation, he sent her away before dawn but not before he had given her six measures of barley, saying, "Go not empty unto thy mother-in-law."

Naomi received the news with such pleasure that we can

almost hear her confiding to Ruth, "The man will not rest until he has finished the thing this day."

She was right. Boaz went before the elders of Bethlehem and challenged the nearer kinsmen to redeem the property and assume his obligations toward Ruth and her mother or to relinquish forever his rights in the matter. The nearer kinsman, while interested in the land, was not willing to accept responsibility for the women. As a confirmation, he loosened his shoe and gave it to Boaz, who then publicly declared his intentions.

The story's happy ending includes the marriage of Ruth and greater blessings than six measures of barley for Naomi. She had lost a husband and two sons; that loss could never be replaced. But the Lord had other blessings in store. Ruth bore a son, and as was the custom in those days, she gave the child to Naomi to care for. Now the same women of Bethlehem who had mourned with her sang and shouted with her, praising the Lord. They declared Ruth was better to Naomi than seven sons.

The child was named Obed. He grew to manhood and became the father of Jesse, who was the father of David. Several generations later, the Savior of the world was born to the house of David in that same city, Bethlehem.

The scriptures repeatedly stress Ruth's Moabite origins. She is presented as both the model daughter-in-law and a member of a shunned idolatrous race. Mosaic law expressly forbade Israelite men from marrying "foreign" women, though Moses himself married an Ethiopian. The concern was that such women would introduce the worship of nature gods; that in fact happened time and again throughout the history of Israel. What made Ruth exceptional was her conversion and devotion to the true God of her husband's people.

Ruth must have been aware of the Israelite attitude toward foreign women. Her faith had already been tried by the triple tragedy that had befallen her good family, all of which Naomi clearly attributed to her God. Her resolve must have been further tested with the drawing back of her sister-in-law, Orpah. In the face of such trials, Ruth chose decisively and forever in favor of her mother-in-law, her way of life, and her God. Her reward was to receive what she did not seek—a husband, wealth, children, and an inheritance among the chosen of Israel.

In the end, there is something appropriate in a Moabite woman's place in the genealogy of Jesus, who was the savior of all the world—every nation, kindred, tongue, and people. I find it even more appropriate that Ruth won that honor by her own faith, and not because of where she was born.

Scripture references:
*Ruth*
Ruth; Matthew 1:5
*Naomi*
Ruth
*Orpah*
Ruth 1:4, 14

# 8

# *Hannah*

When he was an old man, Hannah's son visited the grandson of Ruth, interviewed the young men in his household, and anointed the youngest, David, king of Israel. This presents an interesting connection between the two women, for both at one time despaired of having any children. Ruth had lost her husband and, in traveling to a foreign land, had no way of knowing what the future held. Hannah, like the other barren women portrayed in scripture—Sarah, Rebekah, Rachel, and later Elisabeth— had nearly given up hope of ever conceiving. But Hannah, more than the others, epitomizes the desire for a child.

Childlessness to the ancient Israelites was a tragedy of far-reaching proportions. Israel, as the chosen people, expected to fulfill God's promise, and that meant the bearing and rearing of progeny. Feelings of desperation consumed the pious woman who remained childless. Her lament was not her failure to provide an heir, but that the root of God's people had dried up in her household. It was a condition interpreted by many to be a "shame," a sign of God's displeasure. Isaiah touched on that fear in creating the image of a forsaken, childless woman as he reflected on the destroyed city of Jerusalem. (See Isaiah 54:1-8; also 3 Nephi 22:1-8.) He might have been talking about Hannah, except that her story is almost wholly domestic—an illustration of intimate relationships, including the one between a woman and her God.

A man of the lineage of Ephraim named Elkanah had two wives, Hannah and Peninnah. Peninnah had children; Hannah had none. Every year the family traveled to Shiloh to worship. As part of the ceremonies, Elkanah gave a portion of the offering to Peninnah and a portion to all her sons and daughters. He gave Hannah a "worthy" portion, implying more generosity than was required. Still, because she had no children, her portion was less; it was a painful reminder of her barren condition.

On top of that, Peninnah taunted her. Her husband, seeing her reduced to tears and without appetite, sought to console her, saying, "Why weepest thou? . . . Am I not better to thee than ten sons?"

The scriptures do not say that Hannah was beautiful or gifted, only that her husband loved her. From that I infer that he loved her for herself, her gentle virtues being sufficient, and that it mattered not to him that she was barren. I also imagine that whenever he tried to comfort her, he fanned Peninnah's envy, making her unkind reproaches increase with each year as Hannah's hope diminished.

Caught in that vicious cycle, where could she turn? Hers was no trial of a day, a month, or a year. Each visit to Shiloh must have added to her despair. The very sight of all her fellow countrymen flocking to the observances with their many sons and daughters must have been a cause of great anguish, and the fact that her husband asked why she wept indicates that even he did not fully understand her sorrow. It also suggests that though grieved in spirit, Hannah was not one to rail against Peninnah. Had she told Elkanah of the continued provocations, she might have obtained some relief, but at the expense of alienating Peninnah from her husband and causing domestic strife. Such was not Hannah's character. She sought relief in the one place where it might be found. Taking the words of Moses to heart ("What nation is there . . . who hath God so nigh unto them, as the Lord our God is in all things that we call upon him for?" [Deuteronomy 4:7]), she brought her sorrows to her Heavenly Father.

After the feast, Hannah went alone to the temple. (The place where the ark was kept was called the temple.) There on the steps, she knelt and poured out her soul, fervently weeping.

Her prayer confirms the purity of her character. She spoke from her heart. Before the Lord as before her husband, she did not demand help against the mockery of her rival. She prayed not that Peninnah's joy might be less, but only that she might be considered. Humbly calling herself a handmaid, she placed herself wholly in God's care and with bold confidence made a covenant: "O Lord of hosts, if thou wilt . . . give unto thine handmaid a man child, then I will give him unto the Lord all the days of his life, and there shall no razor come upon his head."

In that manner she vowed to consecrate her child to God as Samson's mother had and as John the Baptist's mother would, his uncut hair being a sign that he was so consecrated.

Even in God's house, she did not find sympathy and understanding. Eli, the high priest, sat by the post of the temple; seeing Hannah praying continually with some agitation, he thought she was drunk and reproved her.

Hannah's defense under his tactless criticism is as ingenuous as her prayer. "No, my lord," she answered. "I am a woman of a sorrowful spirit: I have drunk neither wine nor strong drink, but have poured out my soul before the Lord."

Eli, without knowing her request, added his own prayer to hers and seemingly promised her new hope. "Go in peace," he said, "and the God of Israel grant thee thy petition."

Hannah went her way, and the scriptures add that "her countenance was no more sad." She worshipped with her husband again the next morning, finished the yearly observances, and went home. When her prayer was answered and she gave birth to a son, she named him Samuel, meaning "asked of the Lord."

When the time came again for Elkanah and his family to make their yearly offerings in Shiloh, Hannah asked to be excused, saying, "I will not go up until the child be weaned, and then I will bring him, that he may appear before the Lord, and there abide for ever." Her husband answered that she might do what seemed good to her.

The next verse states that when the child was weaned (from two to three years old), Hannah took him up with her to Shiloh along with three bullocks, some flour, and a bottle of wine. Then "they," meaning Hannah and her husband, slew a bullock and brought the child to Eli. Hannah explained to the high priest that she was the woman he had seen praying and that because the Lord had heard her supplication and granted her the child, she had come to lend the Lord her boy for as long as the child lived.

She had prayed and promised, and when her prayer was answered she quietly redeemed the promise. While the occasion must have been solemn, it was not sad. Hannah, whose vow was at first known only to herself and God, showed no sign of regret, no second thoughts. Before she left Samuel with Eli, this woman, who had prayed with such fervor in her moment of sorrow, offered a prayer of pure poetry in her moment of gratitude.

Hannah's song of thanksgiving distinguishes her as one of the great poets of the Bible. Her ability to express her spirituality in solemnly beautiful phrases evinces constant practice and marks her as a woman of more than modest artistic achievements.

She sang for those who had stumbled but were strengthened; those who were hungry but were fed; those who were barren but now fruitful; those who were low but now lifted up. What Christ would promise his disciples in the Beatitudes, Hannah already knew under the influence of the Holy Spirit.

She affirmed her faith in God, who kept the feet of the righteous on the right road, and offered her testimony of his strength, power, and glory, fully expecting that when the ends of the earth were judged, he would exalt his anointed.

There is no self-exaltation in her song. She doesn't suggest that it was because of any individual merit that her reproach was removed, or that the fervor of her prayer earned God's favor.

She and Elkanah left and returned to their home. Being human, Hannah must have missed her child, his prattle, his clinging attentiveness. How young Samuel was cared for at the temple, the story doesn't say. Other passages in the Bible mention an order of women who devoted themselves to the ministries of the temple; one of these was Anna, who "departed not from the temple, but served God with fasting and prayer night and day."

Whatever the arrangements for his physical care, Hannah must have continued to pray for her son. Evil times prevailed in Israel. Even the tabernacle at Shiloh had questionable caretakers. Eli, though a good man himself, had sons who "lay with the women that assembled at the door of the tabernacle." Knowing that, Hannah must have been concerned as to the effect their example would have on her child. Yet being wise and prudent, she did not inconvenience her whole family by moving to Shiloh to be nearer him. She trusted the Lord, knowing that without his blessing her own means would hardly suffice.

Hannah's trust was rewarded. God revealed himself to the boy Samuel while he was still young, choosing him as a prophet and a judge. Eli, at first slow to perceive the significance of the mysterious voice calling the child by name, accepted God's choice and appointed Samuel to wear the simple linen vest worn by the priests, called an ephod. Hannah, the scriptures say, made with her own hands a long coat of blue fabric for him to wear under the ephod. She brought him a new one each year, at the time of their annual sacrifices, to replace the one he had outgrown.

God blessed Hannah, as well. After Samuel, she had three additional sons and two daughters. More than anything, Hannah had desired a son, and when God gave her one, she gave him back. She did not consider that a sacrifice but a privilege, and she glorified the Lord who had considered her condition and lifted her up. The Lord, in turn, paid her back fivefold.

The story of Hannah illustrates more than one woman's desire for a child. There emerges from between the lines an interesting picture of domestic life a thousand years prior to Christ. The condition of married women among the Israelites during the time of the Judges was relatively free and unrestrained. Hannah, after participating in the religious activities at Shiloh, without imparting her intentions to her husband or asking his consent, went unattended to the temple of the Lord. Had that been uncommon, Eli would have rebuked her presumption or requested that she send for her husband rather than bidding her to "go in peace." Had she not perfect freedom or at least sufficient assurance of her husband's confidence in her decision, she could not have promised the Lord what she had not the power to perform concerning the deposition of her child. In fact, Mosaic law provided a prescribed means by which women could make religious bonds (see Numbers 30:3-16), and Hannah's prayer perfectly illustrates such a pledge. Elkanah's acquiescence throughout shows the high esteem in which he held her. Hannah is credited with bringing the offerings, the bullocks, flour, and wine. She addressed Eli. She sang the song of thanksgiving.

On the day following Hannah's fervent prayer, she went with her husband to worship, suggesting that women as well as men entered the house of the Lord and joined in the services. That the law to attend the observances was binding only on males, possibly because of circumstances that might prevent females, particularly young mothers, from doing so, can be inferred from Hannah's tarrying at home until her child was weaned.

The important point is that Hannah did not think herself unworthy to approach the Lord directly with her problem. The law and the whole history of her people had abounded in God's invitations to pray and in his promises to answer. She went to the Lord because she knew he loved her. Her actions, though based on the traditions of her people, sprang from a deep personal faith. That, too, can be read between the lines.

Scripture references:
*Hannah*
1 Samuel 1; 2:1-21
*Peninnah*
1 Samuel 1:2, 4
*Children promised to barren women*
Genesis 17:16-17; 21:1-3; Judges 13; 1 Samuel 1; 2 Kings 4:14-17; Isaiah 54:1-8; 3 Nephi 22:1-8

# 9

# David's Wives and Their Dilemma

It is romantically appealing to think that women who marry kings have everything and live happily ever after. The truth is more sobering. The life of a queen is complicated by politics, ambition, and court intrigue. She and her children often become pawns in affairs over which they have no control, the outcome of which can mean life or death. Add to that the jealousies of a large harem and numerous sons, all of whom are potential successors to the throne, and the situation becomes even more precarious. David, the second king of Israel, had so many wives, so many of whom faced personal perplexities, that I can't help thinking it was a hazard to be connected to him. Yet these women loved him greatly.

Michal was the first. She met David when he came to play his harp for her father, King Saul, who was suffering from depression and found the music soothing. David is described as being "ruddy," having "beautiful eyes" and being "goodly to look upon." He was an immediate court favorite, not only with Michal, but with her brother, Jonathan, and the king himself, until his jealousy was aroused.

The reward for killing Goliath was supposed to have been Michal's older sister Merab, but David counted being the son-in-law of the king no small matter, and King Saul, considering David a major threat, reneged on his promise and married Merab to another. By that time David was a hero among the people, and Saul's jealousy prompted him to find a way to have David killed. He learned of Michal's love and proposed to use her as a snare, seemingly never doubting that his paternal influence would outweigh his daughter's feelings.

As David was a poor man and could not pay the dowry a king expected for a daughter, Saul proposed that he would give Michal in marriage for the foreskins of a hundred slain Philistines. He expected David to die attempting to satisfy the pledge, but David surprised him. He delivered two hundred bloody foreskins and claimed his bride. That hardly made for an auspicious beginning to a long and peaceful marriage, and, as might be expected, trouble quickly followed.

Jonathan, Michal's brother, tried to foster a truce between David and Saul. David began playing his harp for the king again. Then one day, without warning, Saul threw a javelin and barely missed his son-in-law. David escaped the palace and fled to his own house, but the king sent assassins to overtake him. For Michal it was a tense situation. As long as the truce held, she had managed to keep her father's confidence; now she was forced to choose between her father and her husband. Her decision was complicated by the fact that her own safety was involved.

Michal chose David. She let him down through a window, and he escaped into the darkness while she stalled for time. She had her father's guards take word back that David was sick. Saul ordered that he be brought to him on his bed, so Michal placed one of the household gods in David's bed and covered it with bedclothes. When her deception was discovered, her father railed against her. Confronted with a raving madman, she offered the only defense left her. She said David had threatened to kill her if she didn't help him. Her father, willing to believe any villainy of his son-in-law, accepted her explanation and let her go.

According to the scriptures, Michal "loved David," but she was not to see him again for many years. She would hear that he had sold himself and his sword to Achish, king of Gath, Israel's hereditary enemy. She would learn, too, that he had married again twice—once to Ahinoam, a woman of Jezreel, and again to Abigail. It must have seemed to Michal that he had renounced both his country and his wife. That left her in a curious predicament. She was neither a maid, a wife, nor a widow. She was abandoned.

When her father gave her to another, probably as part of his plot to persecute David any way he could, she seems not to have objected. She went to live east of Jordan with a man named Phalti. The union was illegal, for David was still alive and in no way legally separated from her; but the scriptures indicate that Phalti cared for Michal a great deal.

By the time Saul died, David had acquired what for a man of his circumstances was a large harem. He had six wives, each of whom had borne him a son. Nevertheless, when Abner, the captain of Saul's army, arranged to help David become king, David made the restoration of Michal one of the conditions of the league. Clearly, having Saul's daughter for his wife made David's claim to the throne stronger. That likely was his primary motive. Though Michal loved him and had saved his life, he made no attempt to contact her during all his years as an outlaw. More than once, Jonathan had visited him in secret. David's third wife, Abigail, left her comfortable home to join him and his band of marauders. But there is no word of Michal until he suddenly demands her back as part of the treaty.

She came to Bahurim accompanied by her weeping husband, who was rudely dismissed by Abner. She joined David in Hebron as his first wife, a position of importance. But everything had changed. When he left her window, fleeing for his life, he had been a shepherd boy without a place to call his own, and she had been the daughter of the reigning king. Now the house of Saul was disgraced, hunted, nearly destroyed. If anything, she needed his protection. Time and experience change people. Those who come together after many years' separation are never the same. It is certain that both Michal and David had changed considerably over the years.

With Michal by his side, David ruled from Hebron for seven years. Then he moved his capital to Jerusalem and had the Ark of the Covenant brought up to the city that would bear his name. As he marched into the city at the head of thirty thousand chosen men of Israel, David stripped himself of his royal robes. Wearing only an ephod, he leaped and danced before the newly restored ark. As a musician and a poet, he was immensely susceptible to the significance of the moment. But Michal could not understand his religious zeal. She was embarrassed at what she considered undignified behavior from a king and its possible reflection on her. From that moment, the scriptures say, she "despised him in her heart."

When he returned home, she scorned him. David curtly justified himself, reminding her that he was making merry before the Lord, who had chosen him above her father and all her family. Then follows the phrase, "Therefore Michal the daughter of Saul had no child unto the day of her death." Such a final statement probably indicates that David lived apart from her after their encounter.

Josephus says Michal returned to Phalti and bore him five children, but that seems politically unlikely after David made a point of demanding her as part of his ruling pact.

Most Bible scholars feel that Michal adopted and raised the five orphaned children of her sister Merab. If that is true, she lived to see her five nephews killed.

A famine came upon Israel as a way of reminding David that the actions of Saul had not yet been atoned. A reparation to the Gibeonites was still to be made. The Gibeonites demanded seven of Saul's immediate descendants. David, guided by the Lord, gave them two of Saul's remaining sons and his five grandsons by Merab. They were all hanged.

Michal lived her entire life at the whim of kings during a time when women and their children were often treated as chattel, being bargained for and bought as political expediency dictated. No wonder she grew bitter.

She had taken the initiative in loving the shepherd boy who played the fine music and fought glorious battles. She loved him despite her father's fits of madness and the danger to both their lives. But she could not love the king he became. Through circumstances largely beyond her control, she ended life as a hard-mouthed woman devoid of kin.

Abigail fared better, but only because she kept her wits about her. The scriptures describe her as a woman of beautiful form and good understanding. Her first husband, Nabal, is described as churlish and evil, a drunken wretch, unmanageable, stubborn, and ill-tempered. How Abigail came to be married to him can only be guessed. He was a wealthy man, and likely Abigail's father, in arranging the marriage, gave more thought to his son-in-law's resources than to his personal qualities. How long Abigail had been married to him when David came on the scene is also a matter of conjecture, but it was long enough that she had learned how to manage him in spite of himself.

It was sheep-shearing time, and many guests had gathered at Abigail and Nabal's for the festivities associated with that season. David, who had a band of six hundred men in the wilderness of Paran, sent ten soldiers to ask Nabal for a tribute of food. The future king of Israel, hiding from Saul, lived by levying protection money from the sheep farmers of the fertile plateau, most of whom were happy to pay and would have welcomed David's emissaries, especially inasmuch as David's request was polite and not exorbitant. But Nabal refused; his reply was both contemptuous and insulting.

No sooner had David's men gone than one of the servants told Abigail what had happened. He reminded her that David's request was just and went on to speak rather frankly about the master. Obviously the household had come to rely on Abigail's better judgment.

She lost no time making amends. With the safety of her household at stake, she didn't pause to debate the matter or even to inform her husband. She ordered the baking and packing of two hundred loaves of bread, and she had five sheep dressed and five measures of grain packed. She packed two skins of wine, one hundred clusters of raisins, and two hundred cakes of figs. She sent the foodstuffs ahead; then mounted an ass and followed.

When she met David, he was headed toward her house, armed and determined to raze Nabal's entire establishment. Unafraid, she hastened toward him, alighted from her ass, and humbly interceded for her husband and her household. She sought to lessen Nabal's offense by attributing it not to malice but to folly. She admitted that her husband was a fool and begged David to accept the food and forgive the foolishness. Such folly, she insisted, made him unaccountable and not worthy of David's regard.

Her speech reveals her as a diplomat of the highest order. She makes her case without ever resorting to flattery or forgetting her own dignity. David was impressed, accepted the gifts, and turned back.

When Abigail got home, Nabal was still celebrating. She waited until the next morning, when he was sober, to tell him how near he had come to being slain by David and his men.

The scriptures say that "his heart died within him." Nabal may have been angry at the loss of his goods, the presumption of his wife, or her meddling in his affairs. Or he may simply have been enraged to think that David had bested him after all. Whatever the case, he was dead within ten days.

When David heard of Nabal's death, he praised God for taking revenge in his behalf. Then, after allowing a period of mourning, he sent messengers to ask Abigail to become his wife. Evidently the proposal pleased her, for she "hasted, and arose, and rode upon an ass" straight for his camp.

In marrying David, Abigail exchanged a sedentary life of wealth for that of an anxious wandering band of outlaws. Evidently she considered David's love ample compensation, especially when compared to the wearying annoyances of Nabal's temper. Yet the dangers were real.

Shortly before or just after marrying Abigail, David also married Ahinoam of Jezreel. Then both of these women were captured by the Amalekites, an incident that caused David's followers to consider stoning him. But he inquired of the Lord and was encouraged to pursue his enemies. He recovered the women unharmed.

Abigail lived with David at Gath and was with him at Hebron when he was crowned king. She gave him a son named Chileab or Daniel. Nothing further is recorded concerning her or her son. One thing can perhaps be inferred from that omission. Although her son had a more viable claim to the throne than either Adonijah or Solomon, Abigail made no move to assert it. She was not a part of the palace conspiracy that complicated David's dying days. After her marriage to Nabal, she may have appreciated peace too much to become involved.

Abigail's story is refreshing because she ignored many of the inappropriate social codes of her day, behaving according to her own purposes. She was not about to let her house be razed because of her husband's lack of sense, and when the opportunity came to become the wife of the next king, she wasted no time mourning. Unlike Michal, she did not let her trials and adversities embitter her.

By contrast, Bathsheba seems more pliant. She took no hand in the events in which her life became entangled, apparently making no attempt to either provoke or prevent them. Michal knew David in his youth. Abigail won his heart while he was an outlaw. Bathsheba came into his life after all the winnowing was done. He was king. Jerusalem, which had defied his predecessors, had fallen to him. He had established his capital there and restored the ark. Virtually everything David ever desired came to him, which may explain his downfall. He had come to expect whatever he wanted—and, seeing Bathsheba bathing on her rooftop one day, he desired her.

There is no reason to think Bathsheba was indiscreet in her bathing habits or that she deliberately enticed the king. She came from a God-fearing family and was the wife of a God-fearing man. Indeed, throughout the narrative she maintains the friendship and good graces of Nathan, God's prophet. She was the little ewe with no choice, according to the parable Nathan told David when he exposed the king's guilt. She was simply bathing, performing the ritual ablutions following menstruation, when somehow, unknown to her, she was seen by the king and his passions were excited.

Following that opening scene, we are told, "David sent messengers, and took her." Sarah was twice claimed by a king for her beauty; a braver woman might have refused. Vashti refused King Ahasuerus, as we will see in the next chapter; but refusing a king is risky, as Vashti found out. Bathsheba went to the palace and lay with David.

Some time later, she sent the king a single terse message: "I am with child." At that point David could have arbitrarily claimed her as his wife—certainly a lesser crime than murder, and Bathsheba may even have expected it. She may not have anticipated the murder of her husband, but it is difficult to believe that the possibility of such a course never occurred to her. She simply abdicated her involvement. She saw the problem as David's responsibility and expected him to deal with it.

At first David attempted to cover up his adultery. He called Bathsheba's husband, Uriah, back from the Ammonitish war on a pretext, then insisted that he visit his wife. David sent a feast to his home to help with the festivities. Uriah, rigidly loyal to the law that forbade intercourse to warriors consecrated for battle, slept in the barracks with his men. David, still eager to pass off the child, tried a second time with strong drink. When that failed, he let Uriah carry his own death warrant to the front. David ordered his commander to place Uriah in the thick of the fighting and then to draw back from him.

When Uriah was listed as one of those who had died in battle, Bathsheba mourned. Hers was only the first sorrow, however, for the account is filled with David's remorse. He brought Bathsheba to the palace and made her his wife. Perhaps in his defense, the scriptures later add that "David did that which was right in the eyes of the Lord, and turned not aside from any thing that he commanded him all the days of his life, save only in the matter of Uriah." (1 Kings 15:5.) But that one heinous sin could never be fully erased. Called to repentance by Nathan's parable, David realized the enormity of his sin and flung himself on God's mercy.

Bathsheba's child sickened within a week of his birth. David, in sackcloth and ashes, throwing himself upon the ground, pleaded for the life of his son, but Nathan's prophecy was not to be mocked. The child died. Uttering the poignant phrase "I shall go to him, but he shall not return to me," David went in to comfort Bathsheba.

If Bathsheba didn't know at first, she must have come to know of David's role in her husband's death. How she received that information and reacted to it is not revealed. Did she feel partly responsible? Did she participate in David's repentance? The record doesn't say. We know only that what happened to Uriah and her child didn't paralyze her. She somehow recovered.

Eventually Nathan the prophet assured David that his repentance, as far as was possible, had been accepted. He predicted that Bathsheba's second child, Solomon, would become David's successor. (She also bore him three other sons: Shimea, Shobab, and Nathan.) But the prophet Nathan's earlier prophecy—that the sword would never depart from David's house because he had killed Uriah—was also fulfilled. David lived to see his daughter raped, one son murdered by another, the banishment of his favorite son, and the rebellion of yet another son; finally, he was not allowed to build the temple at Jerusalem.

When David was on his deathbed, Bathsheba intervened at Nathan's request and convinced him to declare Solomon king. She was not his first wife, nor the mother of his favorite son, but she retained enough influence to thwart the plans of her son's rival, Adonijah, who was already amassing support for his own attempt to capture the throne. Her plea in behalf of her own life and the life of Solomon shows wisdom, sophistication, and foresight.

Bathsheba's influence continued into her son's reign. Adonijah appealed to her to intercede for him; he wanted to marry David's concubine, Abishag. Thinking his desire was simply a matter of the heart, she agreed. As she approached Solomon, who was now king, he showed her great respect. He stood and had a chair brought for his mother, then asked her kindly what she wished, promising to deny her nothing. When he heard the request, however, he changed his mind.

Solomon discerned a plot behind Adonijah's petition; his mother was being used. According to Semitic custom, inheriting the women of a dead king was the mark of his successor. Adonijah was trying to solidify his own claim to the throne by marrying David's last concubine. Solomon had him killed.

Abishag, the object of that power play, was present when Bathsheba appealed to David in behalf of her son. She might have been manipulated into either confirming or denying that fact. That made her politically valuable in a double sense.

As David aged, he grew cold. Even covered with many blankets, he could not keep warm. His physicians recommended that a young maid be found to "cherish" him. A maid from Shunem was chosen for her virginity, youth, beauty, and ability to be a practical nurse. The scriptures state that David never knew Abishag in a sexual sense. From Abishag's point of view, that hardly mattered. She would be David's concubine the rest of her life, a prize to be carefully controlled, as Solomon demonstrated when he not only refused his half-brother's request but condemned him for it. We know nothing more about this young woman. Solomon probably incorporated her into his own harem.

David may have had from eighteen to twenty wives and concubines. Ahinoam, whom he married when he was still an outlaw, was carried off by the Amalekites with Abigail and later rescued. She also saw her son Amnon murdered by his half-brother Absalom for raping his sister, Tamar.

Maacah was the daughter of Talmai, king of Geshur. David took her in a battle, and she became the mother of David's beloved son Absalom. Besides seeing her daughter dishonored, she saw Absalom banished and eventually killed.

David's fifth wife, Haggith, was the mother of Adonijah, who won the support of the army in his bid for the throne but was killed by Solomon. Of Eglah and Abital we know only that they were the mothers of Ithream and Shephatiah. If their lives were typical, they knew neither ease nor peace.

One of the punishments Nathan pronounced upon David for his sin with Bathsheba was that what he had done in secret would be done to him before all of Israel. During one of his campaigns against his father, Absalom captured Jerusalem; included in the victory were ten of his father's concubines. He erected a tent on a rooftop and raped all ten in broad daylight, before "all Israel." David was disgraced, but the women suffered considerably more. We are told that when he recaptured the city, he placed his concubines in custody but never saw them again: "So they were shut up unto the day of their death, living in widowhood."

In the Book of Mormon, Nephi's brother Jacob referred

to the tragic fate of David's wives in his powerful denuncia-
tion of polygamy. Insisting that both David's and Solomon's
harems were abominations, he warned his own people
against such practices. The Lord delights in the chastity of
women, he wrote. The Lord has seen the sorrow and heard
the mourning of the daughters of Jerusalem because of the
wickedness of their husbands, and he will not suffer such
practices to continue. Jacob was not referring to a new
problem. Moses, when leading his people out of Egypt,
forbade the taking of many wives (see Deuteronomy 17:17)
and gave concubines the full protection of marriage.

On July 12, 1843, the Prophet Joseph Smith, concerned
with this issue, asked the Lord why Abraham, Jacob, David,
and Solomon, all righteous men, were justified in taking
many wives and concubines. He received the revelation
called the "new and everlasting marriage covenant." (D&C
132.) In that scripture, the Lord explained that though David
had many wives and concubines, he did not sin except in the
case of Uriah's wife, because his wives were given to him
through the prophet Nathan. But because he sinned with
Bathsheba, killing her husband, David fell from exaltation.
We are told that he will not inherit his wives in the next
world, "for I gave them to another, saith the Lord." In light
of that declaration, it is interesting to note that in the
genealogy of Jesus, Bathsheba is called Uriah's wife, not
David's.

The women who intertwined their lives with David's
were individually unique. None were passive acquisitions; i
the larger sense, they were never acquisitions at all. Some
chose David. Most, in one way or another, rose to the
challenges they faced. For that reason, their loss must have
been David's greatest sorrow.

Scripture references:
*Michal*
1 Samuel 14:49; 18:20-28; 19:11-17; 25:44; 2 Samuel 3:13-16;
6:16-23; 21:8; 1 Chronicles 15:29

*Abigail*

1 Samuel 25:3-42; 27:3; 30:5; 2 Samuel 2:2; 3:3; 1 Chronicles 3:1

*Bathsheba*

2 Samuel 11; 12:24; 1 Kings 1:11-31; 2:13-23; 1 Chronicles 3:5; Matthew 1:6

*Abishag*

1 Kings 1:3-4, 15; 2:13-25

*Ahinoam*

1 Samuel 25:43; 27:3; 30:5; 2 Samuel 2:2; 3:2; 1 Chronicles 3:1

*Maacah*

2 Samuel 3:3; 1 Chronicles 3:2 (This woman should not be confused with the name of a city in Syria, three or four men, and several other women of the same name.)

*Haggith*

2 Samuel 3:4-5; 1 Kings 1:5, 11; 2:13; 1 Chronicles 3:2

*Eglah*

2 Samuel 3:5; 1 Chronicles 3:3

*Abital*

2 Samuel 3:4; 1 Chronicles 3:3

*David's concubines*

2 Samuel 15:16; 16:20-22; 20:3

*Marriage discussions in which David's wives are named*

Jacob 2:24-33; Doctrine and Covenants 132 (see especially verses 1, 38-39)

# 10

# *Esther*

The quality of Esther's courage is best appreciated in light of Vashti's. Vashti was the former queen, whom Esther replaced. With character equal to her beauty, Vashti made a stand for modesty. She refused to be viewed as a sex object, and was denounced, dethroned, and divorced. Into that atmosphere came the young girl Esther, probably not more than fourteen years old, concealing a potentially dangerous secret.

The events took place twenty-four centuries ago in the Persian court of King Ahasuerus. He ruled from India to Ethiopia over a kingdom which included the Babylonian territories where the Israelites had been dispersed after the fall of Jerusalem. He was a temperamental tyrant and a lover of finery, including beautiful women. In the third year of his reign, he orchestrated a six-month-long feast. For a hundred and eighty days, he endeavored to impress the nobles and princes of his empire with his glorious opulence. Historians speculate that he may have hoped to win their support for a campaign against Greece. Whatever his reason, the description of the banquet, as given in scripture, impresses us even today. There is mention of wall hangings; fine linen and purple cloth; silver rings; beds of gold; and pavements of red, blue, and black marble.

Immediately following this lengthy festival, the king provided a second feast, this one lasting seven days, for all inhabitants of Persia's capital. On the final day of the festivities, the king, merry with wine, sent seven eunuchs to fetch the queen. Having exhausted all the other splendors at his command, he wished to show off his beautiful wife.

Vashti refused. She would not degrade herself by being made a spectacle before the lascivious Ahasuerus and his drunken satraps, and legally she was within her rights. What the king asked was, by the customs of that time, as indecent as a modern husband proposing that his wife entertain his guests with her naked body. She must have known that given her husband's ego, it was dangerous to risk embarrassing him in front of his guests. And, considering the abject condition of even princes in that day, it seems amazing that Vashti dared to disobey even the drunken command of her monarch. But she did—and the king was enraged.

Amid the constant vying for power and influence surrounding political centers, there are always those ready to take advantage of any opportunity. Several of his princes capitalized on Ahasuerus's anger. Expressing fear that Vashti's refusal would have a disruptive effect on the behavior of women in harems from Persia to Media, they urged him to take action. If Vashti could defy her royal husband, they reasoned, what would happen when whispered news of her impertinence reached the ears of other women in the land? The fear known to all who exercise unrighteous dominion stalked the court of Persia that night, and King Ahasuerus succumbed. He sent out a decree to every province of his empire announcing that Vashti would come no more before him, that her royal estate would be given to another, and that this was done as an example so that every man might rule in his own house, whether great or small.

The next verse hints that in the sobering light of morning, Ahasuerus may have regretted his hasty action. His wife may have meant something to him after all, for the scriptures say that when his anger was appeased, he remembered Vashti. But she had been banished from him, and there was no way the decree could be revoked. So the servants that ministered to the king suggested an alternative as a way to cheer him up. The finest young virgins from all the provinces would be brought to the palace. Each girl in turn, ritually prepared, would spend the night in the king's apartment. The maiden who pleased him most would replace Vashti as queen. Ahasuerus liked the idea and sent out a decree to that effect.

The announcement undoubtedly interested many. In the minds of parents, guardians, generals, politicians, and kings who had been reduced to tributaries, it must have promised a once-in-a-lifetime opportunity. Upon the shoulders of a single lovely girl, a family, a tribe, even a whole subjected nation might find favor. Mordecai must have hoped for such an advantage when he took his adopted daughter, Esther, to the king's chief eunuch and left her in the den of the Persian despot. Why else would he have allowed her to participate in such a beauty contest, knowing Ahasuerus' predilections, unless he felt it was somehow worth the risk?

Mordecai was a Jew, a race so despised that he warned young Esther not to reveal her origins. But perhaps, he reasoned, if Esther won favor, the next king would be half Jewish. So Mordecai took Esther to the king's harem; then each day, without acknowledging his connection to her, he walked outside the house keeping a watchful, loving eye on her.

It was a year before Esther's turn came. On her night, each girl was allowed whatever she wished in the way of perfume and clothing. Esther asked for nothing. She went to the king dressed modestly, unadorned, except with what enhancement her character lent her natural beauty.

The scriptures say that Esther obtained favor with all who looked upon her, and the king loved her above all women. He set the royal crown upon her head. Why the king preferred Esther is not specified. Perhaps he was satiated by mere beauty. Perhaps, too, she shared Vashti's intrepidity—the hint of a spirit unsubdued. Whatever the reason, Esther was chosen. Still, she did not reveal her nationality, though Mordecai sat at the king's gate and she saw him often.

Mordecai, in keeping an eye on his daughter, intercepted some information. Two of those who stood guard at the palace door were planning to kill the king. He passed the information to Queen Esther, who told King Ahasuerus in Mordecai's name. After an investigation, the culprits were hanged, and Mordecai's deed was recorded in the book of the king's chronicles.

Nine years passed. It seems that Esther did not bear a child to King Ahasuerus as Mordecai might have hoped. If a birth had occurred, Jewish historians would have noted the introduction of Jewish blood into the royal Persian line, but no mention is made. Nevertheless, despite rivals within the women's palace, Esther remained in favor until the struggle with Haman.

Haman, an Amalekite, rose to the position of second in the realm, becoming so powerful that the people bowed and reverenced him almost as if he were the king. All honored him except Mordecai, who still sat at the king's gate. The Amalekites were one of the tribes displaced by Joshua when the Israelites entered the Promised Land. Not only were they long-time enemies, but Jehovah had frequently uttered oaths against the sins of that nation. The other courtiers and princes, concealing their envy, did homage, waiting for

Haman to make a false step. They encouraged Mordecai to assume the same attitude and bide his time, but Mordecai's conscience forbade him to bow to a man like Haman. And Haman, though he prospered, became obsessed with this Jew at the gate, who refused to do him homage. He brooded. It would not be enough to lay hands on Mordecai, he decided; he wanted to destroy the entire Jewish race.

Haman went to his soothsayers and cast *purim* (lots) to determine the most propitious day for his scheme. Then he went in and counseled the king. A subversive people scattered throughout the land was the cause of the empire's troubles, he told Ahasuerus, and he magnanimously offered to pay the king for the honor of removing this menace from the kingdom if he could claim the booty. So it was that the first recorded pogrom began.

It is fashionable to speak contemptuously of the disregard with which women were treated in the ancient oriental world. But the offhand manner in which the destruction of an entire race was negotiated by Haman and Ahasuerus shows that women were held no cheaper than men. Human life was expendable. The king answered Haman, "Do as seemeth thee good," and he gave Haman his ring. Using the king's ring to prove his authority, Haman sent notices to every province in the empire. On the thirteenth day of the first month, all Jews, young and old, women and children, were to be killed and their property confiscated.

When Mordecai heard the news, he rent his clothes, put on sackcloth, and entered the city crying loudly. The oriental monarch was accustomed to dwelling in perfect bliss with no sight or sound of human suffering, and for Mordecai to disturb the tranquility of Shushan, the king's royal city, was more than unseemly—it was dangerous. Esther had clothing sent out to him; he refused it. She called her most trusted servant and sent him to inquire why Mordecai was in public mourning. Mordecai returned a copy of Haman's decree and charged her to go before the king and beg for the lives of her people.

Esther sent her servant back to Mordecai with a message reminding him that no one, not even the queen, could go before the king unbidden; that was how assassins approached the throne. There was a law against it, and it was punishable by death. Only if the king held out his scepter would an uninvited supplicant be allowed to live. And the king had not come to her for thirty days. These were not excuses, but the first thoughts of a woman naturally humble, knowing herself to be of an outlawed race and fearing from the long absence of her husband that his heart had been turned against her by her enemies, perhaps by Haman himself.

Mordecai's answer was stern and to the point. He warned Esther that she must not think she was safe from destruction. In a purge, secrets such as hers had a way of leaking out and being used. Still, his most persuasive argument was not based on fear, but on his understanding of the way God worked—an understanding he expected Esther to share. He reminded her that the Jews would be saved—if not by her hand, by some other means. The privileges she had enjoyed for nine years were not hers because she had won them, but by the grace of God. If she held her peace now, she would lose her opportunity to serve and be swept aside. "Who knoweth," he asked, "whether thou art come to the kingdom for such a time as this?"

Even after nine years of wealth, position, and good fortune, Esther was not too proud to remember her humble origins. She was not ashamed of the true God. Her answer embraced all. Gather the Jews living in Shushan, she told Mordecai; fast and pray for me, and I and my maids will do the same. "And so will I go in unto the king . . . and if I perish, I perish."

Would King Ahasuerus really have slain his favorite— his queen? The scriptures indicate that Esther considered her death a real possibility. There was, after all, the memory of what had happened to Vashti, together with a hint that Esther's romantic attraction had waned. Nine years was a long time to remain the preferred beauty in a court where all beautiful women of the land were at the king's command. This time she adorned herself. This time more than just her own fate hung in the balance.

On the third day, Esther entered the palace garden and approached the king. The scriptures say that "she obtained favor in his sight," and he held out his scepter. More than that, he offered her anything up to half the kingdom.

What did she do then? Did she fall to her knees in a muddled state of relief and pour out her request? No. In nine years, Esther had become skilled at court politics. If her confidence in her beauty had waned, her confidence in her wit had not. She proffered, with a lightness oddly incongruent with the danger she had faced, an invitation. She wished Ahasuerus and Haman to dine with her. In this way, she flattered her husband before all the court. Hadn't she risked her life just to see him?

The king and Haman came to her banquet, and again the king asked, "What is thy petition?" Again he offered to grant her any request, even to half his kingdom. She asked only that he return with Haman the following night.

The king agreed, and her flattery worked on Haman as well. He went home to boast to his wife, Zeresh, that no one but he and the king had come to Esther's banquet, and that he was invited again. Then with a bitter tone, he railed, "Yet all this availeth me nothing, so long as I see Mordecai the Jew sitting at the king's gate." His wife offered a solution. Build a gallows, she said, and since you are in such good favor with the king, ask that Mordecai be hanged. Haman ordered a gallows made.

Meanwhile, the king, being restless, called for his book of chronicles. The passage read that night told of the time Mordecai had saved the king's life by exposing the plot of his doorkeepers. The king asked, "What honor hath been done to Mordecai for this?" His servants replied, "There is nothing done for him."

The king asked who was in court. Haman was there; he had returned that very night to ask the king for permission to hang Mordecai. But the king put a riddle to him instead:

"What shall be done unto the man whom the king delighteth to honour?"

Haman, assuming the king meant to honor him, suggested a public display. The man should be dressed in royal attire and mounted on the king's horse; the crown should be placed on his head, and one of the king's nobles should go before him through the town, proclaiming him to the people. The king commanded Haman to take the apparel, the horse, and the crown and so honor Mordecai. Haman complied—with what grace, one can only imagine.

Now, was all that coincidence? Did the king just happen to read of Mordecai's service on the very night when Haman planned to hang him? Surely not. Believing she had risked her life to see him, wouldn't the king have stayed the night with Esther? And doesn't it seem likely that the queen herself picked the passage to be read? Why else would she have played the king along, biding her time, unless she hoped to put into motion events that would strengthen her cause?

The next evening at the second banquet, the king again offered to grant Esther any request to half his kingdom. With the trap so carefully set that Ahaseurus could hardly decide in Haman's favor, when only that day he had publicly honored a Jew, Esther was ready. Yet she remained diplomatic and tactful. She asked for her life and the lives of her people, reminding the king that they had been sold for destruction, and adding that she would not have asked if they had only been sold as slaves.

The king, having been annoyed, forgetful, or drunken when he signed the edict, could not even remember it. Esther explained the plot and who was behind it. Even then, the king hesitated; indecisive, he went out into the garden to consider the matter. Obviously the king liked Haman, but Esther had given him little choice. She had forced Haman to tip his hand, revealing his ambitions when he requested the robes, charger, and crown. By contrast, Ether herself had been offered half the kingdom three times and had requested very little.

Returning from the garden, the king found Haman on his

knees next to Esther's bed, pleading for his life. Choosing to believe that he was trying to force himself on the queen, the king ordered him hung on his own gallows.

The king gave Haman's house to Esther; he gave his ring and the authority that went with it to Mordecai. Then Esther spoke again, falling at his feet and begging the king to undo the command Haman had sent to all the provinces. It was so ordered. In fact, the orders were completely reversed, allowing Jews on the thirteenth day of the first month to take revenge on those who had meant to kill them. The scriptures say that in the royal city of Shushan five hundred men were killed and the ten sons of Haman hanged, specifically at the queen's request.

Modern morality does not condone revenge, especially the kind of revenge Esther took on her enemies. But in the court of Ahasuerus, leniency would have been taken as a sign of weakness and would have undone all that Esther had accomplished. It is to her credit that she sought security for her people, not gain for herself. The scriptures state several times that the Jews took no spoils.

Mordecai, using the king's ring and authority, ordered an annual observance among the Jews—a feast to be called "Purim," because Haman had cast *purim* (lots) to destroy them. The Jews vowed to keep the feast every year from generation to generation. To this day, the festival of Purim is celebrated each March in Jewish synagogues throughout the world.

The story of Esther is so complete, so detailed, and so steeped in romantic drama that some biblical scholars argue that it is fiction. Yet it has held up to historical scrutiny.

There are also those who point out the absence of God's name in the Book of Esther. But the power and presence of Jehovah, the Jews' unseen God, is felt everywhere in the story. That may be precisely the point: providence must often be read backward. Blindly marching forward, we trust that God has some purpose for our lives, that if we listen to his promptings, relying on his strength, he will guide us. But only when we look backward, at where we've been, do we see he was there.

Mordecai suffered the humiliation of seeing Haman rise to power. Esther, at ease amid oriental splendor, found herself suddenly jarred into a new reality. She could choose her course of action; Mordecai pointed that out to her. But if she chose not to be God's instrument for the deliverance of his people, it would mean her own failure, not God's.

The humility in Esther's courage is most moving. She seized her opportunity, employing her intelligence and her honed political skills to cause events far-reaching and bloody. But she never sought to wield such power; rather, faced with the responsibility, she fasted and prayed.

The story of Esther comes from the dark period of bondage when the Jewish national institutions were nearly destroyed. Scattered through Babylon and Persia, the Jews were a nation of captives with no rights, no temple, no altar, and barely any priesthood. In this depressed state, they faced the first pogrom intended to exterminate their entire race. That terrible danger was averted by the beauty, courage, grace, and intelligence of one woman who was willing to acknowledge her talents and advantages as blessings from God, given to her that she might serve him. What is true of Esther is true of all God's daughters. Our gifts, used to serve the Lord, will benefit humankind for generations to come.

Scripture references:
*Esther*
Esther
*Vashti*
Esther 1:9-22; 2:1
*Zeresh*
Esther 5:10-14; 6:13-14

## 11

# *Jezebel, the Witch of En-dor, and Other Wicked Women*

J ezebel is both a name and a label. The name applies to a
woman whose character was hardly sterling. She was
ruthless, politically ambitious, and a worshipper of
idols—a description that might fit half of Israel's kings.
Nevertheless, her name has become the byword, the standard English term for a woman who is shameless and
wicked. How did she come to earn that reputation? Was she
really as evil as her name has come to suggest?

To understand Jezebel, we must appreciate the ancient
religious conflict between worshippers of Jehovah and worshippers of the goddess Ashtoreth and her husband Baal.
Ashtoreth (variously spelled) was represented by a living
tree or a tree-like pole displayed as a symbol of female
fertility. Every Phoenician altar had a representation of
Ashtoreth nearby. The worship of this idol included

immoral sexual rites, thus giving rise to the phrase, "whoring after foreign gods."

When the Israelites first came into Canaan from the desert, they were firm in their faith. They had had forty years in which to solidify their beliefs. Yet many of the generation immediately following those who had invaded the land and settled down to an agricultural lifestyle began to worship the Canaanite nature gods, which were closely associated with farming. If rain didn't fall at the right time or crops failed, it was easy to assume that the local Baalim were angry. Every hilltop had its deities that demanded appeasement to ensure the harvest or the conception of offspring. Before bloodstained altars, the Canaanites and backsliding Israelites indulged in unspeakable rites. Every prophet of that dispensation warned against such idolatrous practices, and every Old Testament mention of Ashtoreth (forty or more times) condemns her. Simply stated, events in the Old Testament can be read as an uncompromising war against nature religion and idolatry in favor of the one true God, Jehovah.

Jezebel has come to epitomize that conflict. She was a worshipper of Ashtoreth, but she was more than just a follower; she espoused and promoted the religion. According to scripture, four hundred prophets of Ashtoreth and four hundred and fifty prophets of Baal ate at her table, indicating that she supported them. She was a powerful advocate of idolatry with a strong following whose very presence threatened the heart of Israel's religion. For twenty-seven years she zealously strove to overthrow the worship of the God of Israel, and she was successful enough to cause even the great prophet Elijah to fear her. This woman's striving against God was the basis for her condemnation—not some vagary or wantonness as the label "a painted Jezebel" has come to imply. Her threat to Israel was on the level of headstrong will, misdirected intellect, and perverted theology.

Jezebel was the daughter of Ethbaal, king of the

Zidonians, a Phoenician kingdom. The Phoenicians were one of the remarkable maritime peoples of the ancient world. They were one of the world's oldest civilizations, controlling a small but immensely wealthy and influential strip of coastal land on the Mediterranean seaboard north of Palestine. By contrast, Israel was still considered an upstart nation. Although David and Solomon had expanded Israel's boundaries, consolidating and increasing its wealth, internal dissension had split the nation in two, reducing the power and influence of both Israel and Judah.

Jezebel's marriage to Israel's King Ahab, which was probably arranged as a political alliance, could not have been considered a worthy match. But Jezebel was not a royal princess who had been sheltered from the bitterness and evil of the world. Her father, who was both the king and high priest of Baal, had murdered his way to the throne. If Israel, a nation still unused to the rule of kings, proved at first disappointing, Jezebel didn't waste any time feeling sorry for herself. She set out to change things.

One of her first acts was to order the extermination of the prophets of Jehovah. These were the priests attached to various villages (see 2 Kings 2:3-5) or who traveled performing particular functions (see 1 Samuel 10:5-13). How many of these devotees of Jehovah she managed to kill, we do not know. We are told only that one hundred were saved. Obadiah, the governor of the royal household, feared the Lord more than his queen, and hid a group of prophets in a cave. One of those saved was Elijah.

In the midst of this religious persecution, Elijah appeared before King Ahab and predicted three years of drought to be followed by a great famine. Elijah made his prophecy, preempting the powers of Baal and Ashtoreth (who were believed to control the weather), and then disappeared. He could not be found, though King Ahab searched frantically throughout all of Israel and sent emissaries to neighboring nations asking for him. Not until at the end of the three years, when the famine had taken full effect, did Elijah appear again. This time he challenged the prophets of Baal to a test atop Mount Carmel—his God against theirs.

The Baal priests had likely performed their ritual, with its attendant magic, many times or they would not have accepted Elijah's challenge. Yet something went wrong and they failed. With taunts and language of unparalleled audacity, Elijah ridiculed the priests of Baal and the impotence of their deities. Then, when it was his turn to perform, he drew lightning from heaven in a triumphant vindication of Jehovah. Swept up in the fervor of the moment, the people, at Elijah's command, seized the failed priests of Baal and massacred all four hundred and fifty.

However, in his triumph, Elijah failed to reckon with Jezebel. She seems not to have been present during the contest, but when she heard of the slaughter of her priests she swore to destroy Elijah "by tomorrow this time." Elijah, who had stood up to the king and single-handedly faced hundreds of Baal priests, fled from this woman's fury. Though he was still under mandate from the Lord, he traveled a day's journey into the wilderness and there implored God to take his life rather than let him fall into the hands of the queen.

The significance of the contest escaped Jezebel. The fact that Elijah had predicted the famine, called fire from heaven, and foretold the return of the rain made no impression on her. She saw only her slain priests and swore revenge.

But she couldn't find Elijah. He had escaped again—this time to Damascus, where he anointed Hazael king of Syria. He also anointed a soldier, Jehu, to be both king of Israel and the destroyer of Ahab and Jezebel's family. Then he selected his own successor, Elisha.

Meanwhile Jezebel, unable to wreak her revenge, set about restoring her religion. She sent for new priests, built more sanctuaries, and, although she stopped murdering the prophets of Jehovah for a time, never ceased hunting for Elijah. Also during this time she sought to teach her husband a lesson on how to be a king.

Ahab's wickedness cannot be blamed entirely on his wife; he was an idolater before he married her. He had distinguished himself as a soldier, but as a ruler he was weak, which gave Jezebel, by her ruthlessness, an advantage over him.

A man named Naboth owned a vineyard next to the king's palace. The palace had been built by Ahab's father, but the vineyard was even older, having been passed down for generations in Naboth's family. From the time Moses first divided the land of Canaan among the tribes of Israel, the Israelites had developed a great respect for property, especially inherited property. Ahab sent for Naboth and asked if he might buy the vineyard, but Naboth made it clear that he intended to pass the vineyard to his son as he had received it from his father. Though bitterly disappointed, Ahab accepted Naboth's answer as being entirely within his rights.

When Jezebel heard of the incident, her view was entirely different. To a Phoenician princess, Naboth's behavior was more than ungracious; it was treasonable. In her country, and in almost every other country ruled by monarchs in that day, *no one* refused a king. She chided her husband; then, taking matters into her own hands, she promised him, like a spoiled child, that she would get the vineyard for him. Having lived in Israel a number of years by that time, she must have been aware of the people's ambivalent attitude toward their rulers. Perhaps she even chose this occasion to strike out against such seeming backwardness. She would not only teach her husband how to rule, but she would teach his people how to be ruled.

She called an assembly and falsely charged Naboth with blaspheming against God and the king. She had him arrested, tried, and condemned by false witnesses she had secured herself. Naboth was stoned and his property seized.

Such highhandedness prompted Elijah's return. As King Ahab strolled through his newly acquired vineyard, the prophet appeared before him. Condemning what Jezebel had done, he told King Ahab that the dogs would lick his blood in that field he had acquired from Naboth, that every male child of his family would be cut off, and that Jezebel would be eaten by dogs near the ramparts of the palace.

King Ahab, offering no argument or rebuttal, tore his clothes and donned sackcloth. The Lord accepted his repentance and delayed part of the retribution. King Ahab, unlike Jezebel, was still capable of remorse.

Three years after its pronouncement, Elijah's prophecy began to be fulfilled. War broke out between Syria and Israel; in the battle, Ahab received a mortal wound. He managed to "stay up" in his chariot until evening to keep the news of his injury from disheartening his forces. Nevertheless he died, knowing his army had been defeated. His bloodstained chariot was taken to a spring running through Naboth's vineyard. There, as it was being washed, a pack of dogs licked King Ahab's blood.

Jezebel survived, unrepentant for another decade. First she concentrated her energies on her son Ahaziah, but he was fatally injured by a fall from a window after he had been king only two years. Jezebel then turned her attention to her second son, Jehoram. He ruled seven years but must have seemed a disappointment to her, for the scriptures make the distinction that although he did evil, his wickedness was not like the wickedness of his mother. What that means is hard to guess, but during a campaign to retake Moab, Jehoram actually went to Elisha, Elijah's successor, to ask advice of Jehovah. Note that he did not send for Elisha, but went directly to him. Elisha spoke to the king with utmost insolence, insulting both his father and his mother. Jehoram did not strike him down or even expostulate. Rather, in the presence of two other kings, his allies in the war, he accepted a public insult to his living mother. Such a betrayal of a woman who prided herself on being queenly must have been crushing. Yet she remained undaunted, seemingly invincible to the end.

Adding further to the insult, Jehu, an army leader who

had been commissioned years earlier by Elijah to overthrow the Ahab dynasty, announced to Jehoram that there would be no peace in Israel so long as the whoredoms of his mother continued. Shortly thereafter, Jehu killed the king and cast his body into the same vineyard that had once belonged to Naboth. Jezebel, hearing of the insurrection and knowing that her death was certain, painted her face and adorned herself as the queen she was. From the tower of the palace, she looked out and awaited the arrival of Jehu. There was no sign of repentance in her as she went out proudly to meet her prophesied doom. The destroyer of her family entered the palace gate, and she shouted down the most insulting taunt she could think of: "Had Zimri peace, who slew his master?"

She knew her words would fall cold and ominous on the ears of Jehu, flushed though he was with victory. Like Jehu, Zimri had been a soldier, a leader of the chariots. Zimri, too, had slain his king and exterminated a royal household. But Zimri's reign had lasted only seven days. Jezebel was insinuating that there would be no peace for Jehu. His time would come, too.

Jehu looked up, and seeing Jezebel's eunuchs on the balcony with her, ordered them to throw her down. Her blood splattered the wall of her ivory-covered palace, and a team of horses trod her underfoot.

Jehu entered the palace, where he ate and drank. Some time later, remembering that Jezebel was a king's daughter, he ordered that she be buried. When the servants went out to bury her, they found only her skull, her feet, and the palms of her hands. The dogs had eaten everything else, as Elijah had predicted.

But Jezebel's death did not put an end to her evil influence. Her daughter, Athaliah, carried her wicked ways into Judah, the southern kingdom of Israel. She was married to Jehoram, the son of King Jehoshaphat, a righteous man who, after many years of strife between the two Israelite nations, probably agreed to the marriage as a political expediency. It was a fatal alliance.

When he was thirty-two years old, Jehoram became king. Athaliah, as her mother had done in the north, promoted the worship of Ashtoreth and Baal among the people of the south. When Jehoram died of an incurable disease (also predicted by Elijah), Athaliah's son Ahaziah assumed the throne. As queen-mother, Athaliah was now more powerful than ever, but within a year, her son was dead. Jehu, the same soldier who had killed King Ahab, murdered Ahaziah. Athaliah, hearing of her son's death and fearing that her own power and influence were at an end, ordered the massacre of all Judah's royal heirs, including her own grandsons. Then she ascended the throne herself. Unbeknownst to Athaliah, however, one of her daughters-in-law had managed to conceal an infant son, Joash, and his life was spared.

Athaliah ruled six years. During her reign, she pulled down part of the temple and used the materials to build a sanctuary for Baal. The people rebelled and rallied around young Joash, proclaiming him the rightful king. Athaliah, hearing the people clapping and shouting, went into the temple and saw the young king. She screamed, "Treason, treason!" but no one came to her aid. Not wanting to defile the house of the Lord with her blood, a temple priest ordered the guards to remove her to a horse gate near the king's house, where she was slain.

The witch of En-dor represents evil of an entirely different ilk. She was a necromancer who wished only to be left alone to practice her art. Actually, the term *witch* is never used in the scriptural narrative describing her; that term has attached itself to her over the centuries. Similarly, it should be noted that she is never described as old, stooped, or hag-like. She has no broomstick, caldron, or tame bird. If anything, the scriptures present her as being rather ordinary, despite the fact that she practiced one of the forbidden arts.

Moses made witchcraft a capital offense, and King Saul, in the early part of his reign, enforced that law by killing those that had "familiar spirits." Later in his life, he fell victim to sin and was afflicted with a deep depression. Faced with both domestic and foreign wars, and being cut off from spiritual counsel, he disguised himself and went to consult the woman of En-dor. He hoped she might induce the spirit of the dead prophet Samuel to revisit the world and submit to questioning.

Like the worship of Ashtoreth and Baal, this aspect of the dark arts was another of the perversions the Israelites had learned from the Canaanites. The prevalence of such practices can be determined by the variety of names in scripture: "sorceries," "consulters of the dead," "seducers," "seducing spirits," "unclean spirits working miracles," "enchantments," "observers of times," "dreamers of dreams," "familiar spirits," "wizards," "diviners," and "charmers," all of which were associated with Satan.

The woman of En-dor knew that what she practiced was punishable by death, and so she was wary of Saul. She listened to his request and made a guarded answer, neither claiming nor denying that she had the ability to call up the dead. Saul pressed her, and the seance began.

It is interesting that although the woman had no ability to see through Saul's disguise, both she and Saul recognized Samuel's shade. She was distressed, declaring that she had seen gods coming up out of the earth.

Samuel called Saul by name and condemned him, predicting that he and his sons would die in battle the next day. Hearing those harsh words, the woman of En-dor sought to comfort her guest. She helped him to her bed and offered him something to eat and drink. Though she was evil, dabbling in Satanic practices, she was not beyond human decency. She was willing to offer aid to one who could not return it.

Isaiah described a time in the last days when the world would be filled with despair, as Saul was. In that time, he says, many will seek the aid of familiar spirits, wizards, and those who "peep" and "mutter." (See Isaiah 8:19.) He warns that those who seek such comfort shall receive little help, remain hungry, and continue to fret.

Saul, when he left the woman of En-dor, though he had rested and eaten, was hardly consoled. She had no power to bless and comfort.

Evil need not always be grand in its proportions. Unlike the other women considered in this nefarious gallery, Herodias operated out of pure personal spite. She wanted John the Baptist killed because he had dared to name her sins.

Herodias was the granddaughter of Herod the Great, who killed the babes at Bethlehem. She married her half-uncle, Phillip I, by whom she had a daughter. (Josephus calls the daughter Salome, though she is not named in scripture.) Herodias then entered into a second, incestuous, and illicit union by marrying her husband's half-brother, Herod Antipas, the Tetrarch of Galilee. Such immorality was an offense to Jewish sensibilities, and it caused some unrest among the people for whom Herod Antipas had responsibility. John the Baptist went so far as to publicly speak out against the marriage. For such boldness Herod had him thrown into prison, but Herod stopped short of taking his life because John the Baptist was popular with the people.

Herodias had no such reservations. She may have felt the threat more keenly. If Herod ever listened to John and repented, her position and power would be imperiled. Her husband had already abandoned one wife, an Arabian princess. Knowing him and his weaknesses well, Herodias encouraged her daughter to dance at his birthday party. With drink flowing freely, Herod, in an expansive mood, promised to reward her with anything she wanted, up to half the kingdom. She consulted her mother; then in the presence of Herod's guests, she requested that the head of John the Baptist be brought to her on a platter.

The narrative states that Herod regretted his oath but could not refuse what he had given publicly. He therefore sent the executioner to the prison to behead the preacher whom he, himself, considered to be just and true. Herodias and her daughter demonstrated no remorse, but we are told that Herod was smitten with fear when he heard of Jesus. He was afraid that John the Baptist had risen from the dead to torment him.

As Jezebel used Ahab to slay the prophets of Jehovah, Herodias used her husband to kill John the Baptist. There the scriptures end her account. Josephus goes on to credit her with her husband's downfall. Jealous of the power of her brother Agrippa, Herodias prodded Herod to demand the title of king. When his request was refused, he was banished. At that time, Herodias could have had her freedom. She refused, choosing to be with the man she loved. In that act of loyalty she evidenced some of the same courage with which Jezebel faced her death.

The qualities of courage, loyalty, and endurance can be possessed by both good and evil women. Not the qualities themselves, but how they are used, make the difference. The verve and vitality of these women have caused some to regard them as sentimentally diabolic, as if the magnitude of their crimes somehow saved them from meaner judgments. Not many individuals can boast, as could the woman of Endor, the distinction of having had a king for a client. Athaliah, in her wholesale massacre, nearly exterminated the lineage of David through which the promised Messiah was to come.

I have read a vindication of Jezebel in which she was portrayed as a woman of high character who zealously devoted her life to religious reform. It just happened that her god was Phoenician rather than Hebrew. It is true that Jezebel was not, as the dictionary says, a shameless or wanton woman. Her crimes were not of that order. Still, it seems impossible to justify her character, for her wickedness ran deeper than the mere practice of idolatry. Indeed, the scriptures identify many idol-worshippers who were highly ethical: Naomi was treated well by the Moabites. Pagan sailors aboard the ship carrying Jonah treated him decently. Pharaoh's daughter risked her father's wrath to save Moses. Naaman, the Syrian, took advice from his wife's Israelite maid. And a Zidonian widow, one of Jezebel's own people, fed Elijah during the long famine.

Any attempt to glamorize these women is a misrepresentation, as is reducing them to labels or attributing their actions to their environment. Dancing is not evil because Herodias used her daughter in that fashion; neither is wearing makeup sinful because Jezebel painted her face to meet Jehu. The wicked women in scripture are evil because of specific and willful acts, not by chance associations. If that were not true, the concept of personal accountability would be invalid.

Scripture references:
*Jezebel*
1 Kings 16:31-34; 18; 19; 21; 22:37; 2 Kings 9:7-37; see also Revelations 2:20
*Ashtoreth (sometimes translated as "grove" or "green tree")*
Exodus 34:13; Deuteronomy 16:21; 23:18; Judges 2:11-13; 6:25-30; 10:6; 1 Samuel 7:3-4; 12:10; 31:10; 1 Kings 11:5, 33; 15:13; 16:33; 2 Kings 13:6; 17:16; 21:3-7; 23:4-7, 13-15; 2 Chronicles 15:16; Isaiah 17:8; 57:4-5; Jeremiah 7:18; 17:2; 44 (entire chapter); Ezekiel 13:18; 3 Nephi 21:18
*Athaliah*
2 Kings 8:26; 11:1-20; 2 Chronicles 22; 23:12-21; 24:7 (Athaliah should not be confused with two men of the same name; see 1 Chronicles 8:26; Ezra 8:7)
*Woman of En-dor*
1 Samuel 28:3-25. See also Leviticus 19:31; 20:27; Exodus 22:18; Isaiah 8:19
*Familiar spirits, witches, witchcraft*
Exodus 22:18; Leviticus 19:31; 20:6, 27; Deuteronomy 18:10-11; 1 Samuel 15:23; 2 Kings 9:22; 21:6; 23:24; 1 Chronicles 10:13; 2 Chronicles 33:6; Isaiah 8:19; 19:3; Micah 5:12; Nahum 3:4; Acts 16:16; Galatians 5:20; 2 Nephi 18:19; 3 Nephi 21:16; Mormon 1:19; 2:10; Doctrine and Covenants 46:7
*Herodias and her daughter*
Matthew 14:3-12; Mark 6:14-28; Luke 3:19-20

## 12

# Two Temptresses: Delilah and Potiphar's Wife

T he obvious difference between Delilah and Potiphar's wife is that one got her man and the other didn't. Beyond the obvious, there are other differences. Delilah was a Philistine living on the border of Canaan and working for money; Potiphar's wife was an upper-class Egyptian who enjoyed the privileges of her husband's station but wanted more pleasure.

Men and women alike have an acculturated notion of the "temptress." We expect her to be spoiled, sensual, and selfish. From the scriptures we can be sure of only one common trait: determination. The single-minded determination of both Delilah and Potiphar's wife may have as much to do with their enduring notoriety as did their sensuousness.

Potiphar's wife tempted Joseph "day by day." Her

passion was not a sudden flare of lust; it grew slowly, gathering momentum as her insistence increased.

From the time Joseph first arrived in Egypt as a young boy, he served Potiphar. The scriptures indicate that God was with Joseph and prospered him, and through him blessed those he served. Potiphar noticed that the boy seemed favored; and he made him overseer of increasing portions of his affairs until Joseph could say with honesty that Potiphar kept nothing from him but his wife.

Being the favorite was a role Joseph understood and played well. He may have inherited his mother's comeliness; he most assuredly possessed his father's ability to turn adversity to advantage. Uprooted from his pastoral home and transplanted to a large household populated by women, eunuchs, slaves, and servants, where intrigue, chicanery, nepotism, and sycophancy were common, he not only survived but rose to the top. Joseph was a slave still, but a slave with authority. His good fortune, however, was not an unmixed blessing. It brought him to the attention of Potiphar's wife, and she had designs on him.

We know nothing of the woman's age or appearance, and we can only guess at her motive. Potiphar, as captain of Pharaoh's guard, may have been elderly or young, fat or thin, cruel or indifferent. None of that would have been considered when the marriage was arranged. A man of his position would have the wife of his choice; she would have less say in the matter. If she ever loved him, her love must have been less than complete if she was seeking daily to seduce Joseph.

Potiphar's wife saw a provocative body and a character that inspired respect, but she had no insight into Joseph's spirit. She knew nothing of the sacred covenant God had made with his race, or of the young man's own visionary dreams. How well Joseph had adapted to the Egyptian way of life is shown in the fact that he shaved. (See Genesis 41:14.) In the thousands of tomb and temple paintings extant from ancient times, Egyptian males are always clean-shaven, while barbarians and inferior races are bearded. The fact that Joseph had adopted that custom, together with the custom of wearing a white linen garment, must have made him appear Egyptian. Potiphar's wife may have expected him to be Egyptian in his morals, as well.

Potiphar's wife made the first advance. Joseph wasn't allowed the luxury of passion; a slave was expected to be as sexless as a eunuch. Such detachment, in such close and daily proximity, must have been a torment to the woman in love. She may have felt that nothing but their difference in station stood between them and that she had but to cast that barrier aside. One day, when they were alone, she, one of the most prominent women in all of Egypt, offered herself to her slave.

Joseph's prompt answer may betray how close she came to a correct assessment of his situation. Her offer was doubtless tantalizing to this young man cut off from normal female society; and, if he harbored any resentment for his servile position, the satisfaction might have been temptation enough. He could have cuckolded the man who owned him. But there was a side to Joseph less evident to Potiphar's wife than his sexuality. His response to her provocation, revealing that side of him, must have shattered her with its honesty. What she viewed as a romance, he termed a "great wickedness."

She chose not to hear. Within the conventions of her position, she was accustomed to having her own way. She persisted, wearing at him, deluding herself that she had only to overcome some shyness in him.

He continued to refuse her day by day. Then came the moment when all possible obstacles were removed. The husband was gone, as were the servants. When Joseph came into the house on business, she embraced him and held him fast. She may have hoped that her flesh touching his would at last overcome his hesitation. Not bothering with his usual excuses, Joseph wrenched himself free, leaving his outer garment behind.

That final demonstration of his self-mastery may have turned her lust to scorn, or it may simply have been fear that prompted her next action: "When she saw that he had left his garment in her hand . . . she called the men of her house." The garment would have been difficult to dispose of, impossible to explain. With no time for reflection or subtlety, she screamed. She told her story first to the other male servants of the household and then to Potiphar. Joseph, she insisted, had tried to rape her. She resisted and he fled, leaving his garment behind.

The story was believed—and why not? Graciously condescending, Potiphar's wife identified herself with her servants, speaking of the "Hebrew brought in to mock us." To her husband she spoke arrogantly of the "Hebrew servant" who had been presumptuous. Potiphar was a man of the world; he knew the weaknesses of men. Besides, the garment served as proof.

Potiphar had Joseph thrown into prison. Joseph submitted without offering any defense; there is no record of his speaking out against his accuser. Defense would have been futile, as he must have known. But he could have sown seeds of doubt in Potiphar's mind, if he had so desired.

Nothing more is said of Potiphar's wife. She serves more as a symbol of the faithless wife than as a fully rounded individual. The narrative sweeps on to Joseph's triumph. Within two years he rose to be second in power only to Pharaoh.

Delilah, on the other hand, was no frail sinner suffering from too much love. She was the artful manipulator of men's passions, who could achieve her ends without ever experiencing a throb of true emotion herself.

Samson was a judge in Israel at a time when his nation, because of its unrighteousness, had fallen under domination by the Philistines. Since before his conception, when an angel announced his birth to his mother, he had been consecrated to the Lord; his uncut hair was the symbol of that vow. He had also been endowed with enormous physical strength. Samson might have led his nation out of sin and bondage, but he never showed any inclination to undertake such a mission. Instead, he squandered his powers in ridiculous and dangerous adventures.

Samson desired a Philistine woman and instructed his parents to arrange the marriage. They objected, reminding him that she was a foreigner, but Samson's wishes prevailed because she pleased him. He married her and immediately through her became a victim of the Philistines.

Samson was a frolicsome giant and a great jokester. During the merriment of the wedding festivities, he proposed a riddle that he had himself invented, offering to pay his Philistine guests in linen garments if they came up with the right answer; otherwise, they must pay him. No one could guess it. After several days of wrong guesses, the young Philistines threatened Samson's new wife, who then wept until at last she wearied him. He had no sooner told her the riddle's solution than the Philistines knew it.

Angered, Samson waylaid other Philistines, took their robes, paid his debt, and returned to his parents' house. His new wife, abandoned, was given by her father to Samson's best man. At harvest time, Samson went to visit his bride, only to have her father explain that he had given her away because he thought Samson hated her. He hinted that her younger sister was fairer anyway, but Samson didn't warm to that idea.

Instead, he tied torches to the tails of three hundred foxes and set them loose in the Philistines' fields, burning their crops. A minor war ensued. In revenge, the Philistines burned Samson's wife and her father. Samson retaliated by slaying a thousand men with the jawbone of an ass. His enemies tried to bind him, but Samson could not be bound. One night when his enemies tried to capture him, he defied them by carrying off the gates of the city—doors, posts, bar, and all.

If the Philistines didn't know where Samson's strength lay, they knew his weakness. They offered Delilah eleven hundred pieces of silver to discover how he could be subdued. That was an enormous sum; Judas betrayed Jesus for only thirty pieces of silver.

The Bible describes Delilah as a woman living in the valley of Sorek, leaving her nationality and livelihood vague. Josephus states plainly that she was a Philistine harlot, and everything about her story suggests that she was a courtesan of unholy persistence who had personal charm, mental ability, self-confidence, and considerable nerve. It might be argued that from the Philistine point of view, she was a patriot who betrayed Samson for the sake of her people, but the evidence suggests otherwise. Delilah was consistent; she used her abilities for one purpose — money.

The chapter introducing Delilah begins, "Then went Samson to Gaza, and saw there a harlot, and went in unto her." That woman was not Delilah, but the mention of the harlot reveals the nature of Samson's habits. The experiences following his unfortunate marriage had not cured him of his love for Philistine women. He was not a welcome visitor in Philistine cities — his visits were made at some risk — yet he persisted. The scriptures go on to say that eventually Samson came to love a woman named Delilah. The rest of the story reads like an allegory, so exactly does it describe the downfall of a man enslaved by his own passions.

Samson could not possibly have cherished any illusions about Delilah. He had already been betrayed by a woman of her nationality, and many of her actions would have aroused suspicion in any lover. But unlike Joseph, who fled his temptress, Samson was confident. He didn't fear her. Instead, he dallied with temptation, trifling with sin, allowing himself to be brought ever nearer to destruction as Delilah plied him with her charms.

Delilah was skillful, to be sure. "Tell me, I pray thee, wherein thy great strength lieth," she cooed. He jokingly answered that if she were to bind him with seven undried withs (new cords), he would be weak like other men. When she tried it, he flexed his muscles and laughingly threw off his bonds. Try new ropes, he suggested. When they failed, he let her weave his long hair into her loom. For Delilah, with a fortune in silver at stake, the game was serious. But for Samson, the episodes were light, playful interludes in their more serious love-making.

At last, bored or simply not in a mood for sport, he told her the truth. He was a Nazarite. His hair had never been cut. That, he believed, was the source of his strength.

Perhaps his three victories over the Philistines, together with his threefold resistance to Delilah's wiles, had made him feel invincible. On the other hand, he enjoyed flirting with disaster. Perhaps he believed that even cutting his hair would not weaken him.

Now the tone of the narrative changes. Delilah didn't run for her scissors the way she had run for the withs, ropes, and loom. She knew her man, and she knew she had the truth. Not mentioning the secret again, she entertained him for the evening. When he left, she sent for the Philistine lords and demanded her money.

The next time Samson came, she enticed him to put his head in her lap. She soothed him to sleep, then sheared him. She gave those with whom she had bargained exactly what they had bargained for: she delivered Samson powerless into their hands. And, like Potiphar's wife, she escaped unpunished. Nothing in scripture indicates that she suffered any remorse, repentance, or retribution.

There is something heartrending in the spectacle of Samson, once the lighthearted giant, now blind and helpless, chained to a Philistine grindstone. Whatever pity he inspires may be the reason he is often portrayed as the victim of both his first wife and Delilah. I question that representation. Samson took pleasure in visiting brothels and in killing his enemies. He is nowhere presented as a man of integrity, and neither he nor Delilah evidence much virtue. They were essentially responsible for their own downfalls. That is as it should be, according to the doctrine of free agency.

Yet few dangers are more dramatized in scripture than

the power of a seductive woman. Nearly always when idolatry was introduced among the Israelites, it was blamed on the arts and devices of heathen women. The image of a harlot is used to describe Israel's unrighteousness by Ezekiel, Hosea, Amos, Micah, Jeremiah, and Nahum. The verb "to play the harlot" is synonymous with apostasy in Exodus, Leviticus, Numbers, Deuteronomy, Judges, 2 Kings, the Chronicles, Psalms, Proverbs, Isaiah, and the New Testament (particularly in Revelation). The Book of Mormon also picks up Isaiah's image of erring women and dubs the abominable church of the last days "the whore of all the earth."

One might think from these numerous references that in some periods of Israel's history most women were engaged in wanton practices. Such was never the case. Many of these references apply to specific sexual ceremonies incorporated into the worship of idols, Ashtoreth in particular. These practices were especially abhorred by the prophets of God and came to be used metaphorically to represent all evil.

God instituted sex when he created the male and the female, and he pronounced it good. He added that a woman's desire for her husband would be as great as his desire for her. Likewise, men can tempt women as surely as women tempt men. The story of Potiphar's wife demonstrates that chastity is as important in males as in females; and Samson's debacle illustrates the fact that no man can be corrupted who isn't already corruptible.

Human sexuality is a potent force. Lust creates real problems, and unquestionably evil women of all ages have found their seductive powers useful. However, righteous women use their sexuality to add grace and charm to their lives. Fortunately, most women in every age have used their sexuality to procreate families and to please themselves and their spouses—the purposes for which God has created it. Every person must thus learn to recognize the power of his or her sexuality and decide to use it only for those righteous purposes.

Scripture references:
*Potiphar's wife*
Genesis 39:8-19
*Delilah*
Judges 16:4-21
*References to harlotry*
Exodus 34:15-16; Leviticus 17:7; 20:5-6; Numbers 14:33; 15:39; 25:1; Deuteronomy 31:16; Judges 2:17; 8:27, 33; 2 Kings 9:22; 1 Chronicles 5:25; 2 Chronicles 21:13; Psalms 73:27; 106:39; Proverbs 6:26; 7:10, 27; 23:27; 29:3; Isaiah 1:21; 23:15-16; 57:3; Jeremiah 2:20; 3:1-9; 5:7; 13:27; Ezekiel 6:9; 16:15-41 (elaborate metaphor); 20:30; 23 (entire chapter is an elaborate metaphor); 43:7-9; Hosea (entire book is an elaborate metaphor); Amos 7:17; Micah 1:7; Nahum 3:4; Matthew 21:31-32; Luke 15:30; 1 Corinthians 6:15-16; Ephesians 5:5; 1 Timothy 1:10; Hebrews 13:4; Revelations 17:1-16 (elaborate metaphor); 19:2; 21:8; 22:15; 1 Nephi 13:7, 34; 14:10; 22:13; 2 Nephi 9:36; 10:16; 13:16-26; 26:32; 28:14, 18; Jacob 2:23, 28; 3:5; Mosiah 11:2, 6, 14; Alma 1:32; 30:18; Helaman 6:23; 3 Nephi 16:10; 21:19; 30:2; 4 Nephi 1:16; Mormon 8:31; Ether 10:11; Doctrine and Covenants 29:21; 63:17; 86:3

# 13

# *Mary, the Mother of Jesus*

When the season rolls around again and I find myself setting out the nativity figures under the Christmas tree, when I wipe the dust from the folds of her gown and place her in the center with the manger in front and Joseph to one side, I think about Mary. For a brief moment, she was the central figure in the greatest drama of all time, the giving of the Christ child. The angel Gabriel said of her, "Blessed art thou among women." Indeed, she was the long-awaited virgin who conceived miraculously and brought forth the Son of God—a divine promise of atonement for humankind. No woman had been more honored or revered, and rightly so. Yet Mary's glory flows not entirely from the events that happened to her, but from the way she responded to God.

From Nephi's vision (1 Nephi 11:13-15), we know that

Mary was foreordained to the role she played. She must have been one of the most valiant of all spirits to have been entrusted with the nurturing, care, and cherishing of the Savior. But the real inspiration is her humanness—her natural reactions to the events that surrounded her.

While Mary was still very young, an angel appeared. Seeing him, she was troubled, wondering what this vision might be. Luke writes, "And the angel said unto her, Fear not, Mary: for thou hast found favour with God. And, behold, thou shalt conceive in thy womb, and bring forth a son, and shalt call his name JESUS. He shall be great, and shall be called the Son of the Highest: and the Lord God shall give unto him the throne of his father David: and he shall reign over the house of Jacob for ever; and of his kingdom there shall be no end. Then said Mary unto the angel, How shall this be, seeing I know not a man?"

Undoubtedly Mary knew the traditions of her people. She knew that a Messiah was to be born, and she must have understood that to be the mother of the Savior would be the highest honor ever to come to a woman. Her lineage was correct; perhaps she had even contemplated the possibility of such a blessing coming to her. If so, at that moment when she talked to the angel, she brushed all speculation aside and went right to the heart of the matter—her purity. She was a virgin, and so with clear, uncluttered instincts she questioned the birth. How could this be?

Only after the angel explained did Mary submit her purity to the cause, declaring, "Behold the handmaid of the Lord; be it unto me according to thy word." If she realized that her obedience might mean disgracing herself and her espoused husband, that it might mean being banished from her home or condemned as an unwed mother, she gave no indication of her fears. She was willing to serve God.

Shortly after the angel's visit, Mary traveled some distance to see her cousin Elisabeth, who was in her sixth month of pregnancy. The angel had told Mary of Elisabeth's great joy, but Elisabeth had no way of knowing Mary's except as it was revealed to her. Luke tells us that Elisabeth, on seeing Mary, felt the babe leap within her. Being filled with the Holy Ghost, she bore witness to the divine mission of Mary's child, repeating the angel's words "Blessed art thou among women."

Mary, too, was touched by the Holy Ghost. The young, ingenuous girl who had spoken so plainly to the angel exclaimed her joy and gratitude in poetry. Echoing the Psalm of Hannah, with which she must have been familiar, she expressed her depth of feeling at being chosen:

My soul doth magnify the Lord,
And my spirit hath rejoiced in God my Saviour.
For he hath regarded the low estate of his handmaiden: for, behold,
    from henceforth all generations shall call me blessed.
For he that is mighty hath done to me great things; and holy is his name.
And his mercy is on them that fear him from generation to
    generation.
He hath shewed strength with his arm; he hath scattered the proud
    in the imagination of their hearts.
He hath put down the mighty from their seats, and exalted them
    of low degree.
He hath filled the hungry with good things; and the rich he hath
    sent empty away.
He hath holpen his servant Israel, in remembrance of his mercy;
As he spake to our fathers, to Abraham, and to his seed for ever.

Then the exalted moment passed. The visit ended, and Mary returned home to await the time for giving birth.

It soon became known that Mary was with child. We might well imagine the consternation such a report brought to those who loved her, and to Joseph especially. His love and respect were evident in his response. He could have openly shamed her; instead, he determined to put her away privately with a writ of divorcement.

While he grieved over this matter, an angel appeared and told him not to be afraid to take Mary as his wife. The angel explained that Mary's pregnancy was the fulfillment of prophecy, that "a virgin shall be with child, and shall bring forth a son, and they shall call his name Emmanuel, which being interpreted is, God with us."

Joseph accepted the angel's message and took Mary as his wife. The days that followed, while Mary and Joseph waited for God's son to be born, must have been marvelous. This young couple understood God's purpose for their lives, and they knew of his great confidence in them.

On the night the child was born, heavenly choirs confirmed the glad tidings. Shepherds in the fields, hearing, came to see the babe whom Mary had wrapped in swaddling clothes and laid in a manger. Luke records the event: "And they came with haste, and found Mary, and Joseph, and the babe lying in a manger. And when they had seen it, they made known abroad the saying which was told them concerning this child. And all they that heard it wondered at those things which were told them by the shepherds." Luke adds, "But Mary kept all these things, and pondered them in her heart."

Mary held in her heart the intimations of divine significance, pondering them. Seemingly, she, like most of us, struggled to comprehend. Yet she never faltered, and continued to display great wisdom and spiritual discernment in the events that followed.

As was the custom, she and Joseph brought the child to Jerusalem and presented him at the temple. There they found a man named Simeon. According to Luke, the Holy Ghost was upon this just and devout man, who had been promised that he would see the Messiah before his death. Taking Mary's child into his arms, he exclaimed, "Lord, now lettest thou thy servant depart in peace, according to thy word: for mine eyes have seen thy salvation, which thou hast prepared before the face of all people; a light to lighten the Gentiles, and the glory of thy people Israel."

Again Mary had received a confirmation, and yet "Joseph and his mother marveled at those things which were spoken of him."

Still filled with the Holy Ghost and perhaps perceiving the young couple's confusion, Simeon went on to bless Mary and Joseph saying, "Behold, this child is set for the fall and rising again of many in Israel; and for a sign which shall be spoken against; (yea, a sword shall pierce through thy own soul also,) that the thoughts of many hearts may be revealed."

Simeon's witness carried with it the foreshadowing of Mary's own anguish as he prophesied of events to come. Then his testimony was supported by yet another witness—Anna.

Anna was a widow who never left the temple "but served God with fastings and prayers night and day." She came up, gave thanks, and spoke of this babe as the one promised for redemption in Jerusalem.

With these testimonies ringing in their ears, Joseph and Mary left the temple with the child. Soon wise men from the East sought them out and bore yet another witness. Then, being warned by an angel, the young family fled to Egypt. Finally they returned to Nazareth, where in their care and company Jesus grew.

The scriptures record almost nothing about Christ's youth. But as a mother, I can imagine how it must have been for Mary. From the time they were born, I have watched my own children develop in delightfully unexpected ways. So it must have been with Jesus. Christ's wisdom and grace must have been a steady, daily unfolding to Mary.

We, on the other hand, are given only a glimpse of the boy some twelve years later in Jerusalem, where the family had gone to be taxed. Jesus was found to be missing, and after three days of searching was located in the temple. On finding the lad his mother scolded him, saying, "Son, why hast thou thus dealt with us? behold, thy father and I have sought thee sorrowing."

Surely Mary must have understood that God would not allow anything to happen to his Son. He had an important mission yet to perform. But, like any mother, she worried.

Jesus' answer was revelatory: "How is it that ye sought me? wist ye not that I must be about my Father's business?"

With those words, the magnitude of this young man's

divine parentage was revealed. He was growing up; he was making known his feelings concerning God. And again Luke records that "his mother kept all these sayings in her heart."

Mary had conversed with an angel. While still a virgin, she had miraculously conceived and given birth. She had received numerous witnesses testifying to the divinity of her child. She herself had prophesied under the Holy Ghost's influence. And yet, she continued to marvel and to ponder.

That, I think, is the significance of Mary's life: it manifests the workings of faith. She had been given to know a great deal, but she had to grow into an understanding of what she knew. It is to her credit that she had the initial humility to respond to her unusual call from the Lord, and it is noteworthy that through the years she continued to serve. But only gradually, as she fleshed out the skeleton of her own experience, did her understanding become complete.

By the time of the marriage at Cana, Mary knew that Jesus could change the water into wine, and she asked him to perform the miracle for her. She expected that he would grant her request and told the servants to do as he said.

No doubt Mary's increased faith and understanding became the "sword" of sorrow that would pierce her soul as Simeon had prophesied. Following the marriage at Cana, she was to watch her son take up and fulfill his divine mission. No mother ever hopes to have a son rejected, denied, and crucified; and certainly knowing that son to be the Savior of the world, the promised Messiah, the Son of God, could only have intensified Mary's pain.

One day Jesus sat in a house surrounded by his disciples. When someone came to inform him that his mother and brethren were outside seeking him, he replied, "Who is my mother? and who are my brethren? . . . Whosoever shall do the will of my Father which is in heaven, the same is my brother, and sister, and mother." (Matthew 12:48, 50.) Like all children, Jesus first learned love from the nurturance he received from his mother. For him to liken that bond to his love for all who serve God was a high tribute to Mary. And he was deeply concerned for her welfare. As he hung on the cross in his final hour, he looked down and commissioned the apostle John to care for her; and "from that hour that disciple took her unto his own home." (John 19:27.)

Mary was active in the early Christian church. The final mention of her is found in Acts 1:14, where we are told that she gathered with the apostles in the upper room in Jerusalem. I imagine that following the Resurrection Mary had new miracles to ponder and new work to do as a special witness of her son's divinity.

Yet when all is told, we still don't know many details about Mary. Did she have a fine voice? Did she enjoy sewing? Were there flowers in her garden? Perhaps, but what does that matter? We know the important things about her. We know Mary loved what was good; we know she was obedient; we know she raised her son to adulthood and then had the wisdom to relinquish her role and allow him to perform his mission under his Father's spiritual guidance. We know that she stood by him. She was nearby when he was teaching. She mourned him at the cross. She was always there, never attempting to draw attention to herself but quietly adding her witness.

Mary was a partner with God in a unique sense. But each of us, Mary included, has another kind of partnership with God—a partnership rooted in experience and the righteous use of agency. As a young girl, Mary gave herself to be "the handmaid of the Lord," but only after she had lived and loved and struggled did she begin to understand what the angel meant when he said, "Blessed art thou among women." Mary, for all her favor with God, still had to give herself to God to fulfill his purposes, as we do.

Scripture references:
*Mary*
Matthew 1:16-23; 2:11; 13:55; Mark 3:31-35; 6:3; Luke 1:27-56; 2:16-48; John 19:26-27; Acts 1:14; Mosiah 3:8; Alma 7:10; 19:13
*Anna*
Luke 2:36-38

# 14

# *Elisabeth*

What mother hasn't dreamed great things for her child? And if the child is an only child, a long-awaited child, how much more does it become the center of ambitions, hopes, and dreams?

When the angel Gabriel announced the birth of John, he promised Zacharias that the son his wife conceived would be great, a leader, full of the Holy Ghost from his mother's womb. But he would not be the greatest of leaders; that honor belonged to the child of his wife's cousin. Knowing this, how did Elisabeth greet Mary? With envy? No. She welcomed her cousin with open arms, readily acknowledging Mary's great honor, glorying in the Lord and saying, "Whence is this, . . . that the mother of my Lord should come to me?"

Elisabeth had prepared all her life for the role she was to

play. As a descendant of Aaron and the wife of a priest, her activities centered around the temple. Though aged and childless, which may have lessened her esteem among her peers, she was blameless before God, having kept all the commandments and ordinances. Yet for many years her prayer for a child had remained unanswered.

Then the lot fell to Zacharias. During his week to officiate in the temple, each priest scrupulously maintained his worthiness; but inasmuch as over fourteen hundred men might participate, and the selection of a single priest who would enter the Holy Place to burn incense was determined by the drawing of a lot, that honor might never come, or might come only once in a lifetime. When the lot fell to Zacharias that day, it was honor enough. But a vision was opened to him, as well.

He beheld an angel standing on the right side of the golden altar. Zacharias was troubled, afraid. But the angel said, "Fear not, thy prayer is heard." Which prayer? It was obvious: the one Zacharias had uttered until his hope had turned to ashes, the one his wife still offered continually, even though to keep asking seemed a mockery. The angel stated it clearly: "Thy wife Elisabeth shall bear thee a son." His promise went further: the child was to be a blessing to the people, a cause for rejoicing, the means of turning many souls to God. He would go before in the Spirit of Elias to make ready a people prepared to receive their Lord.

Doubtless Zacharias recognized in those words the great forerunner of whom the prophets had spoken, but it was more than he could believe. How, he asked, could he know that what was spoken was true? He was an old man, and his wife was well stricken with years. The angel (the prophet Elias, according to Doctrine and Covenants 27:7) reiterated the authority by which he had come to bring those good tidings. Then, for a sign, he struck Zacharias dumb, rendering him speechless until that day when all would be fulfilled.

Many people waited outside the Holy of Holies. As was the custom, they watched for the clouds of incense smoke to appear above the great partition that separated the general assembly from the Holy Place. Zacharias was a long time in the temple that day, and when he reappeared, he was unable to pronounce the benediction. He beckoned, and by signs he made it known that he had seen a vision.

When the days of his ministrations in the temple were completed, he returned to his home. There his wife conceived and hid herself for five months, saying, "Thus hath the Lord . . . looked on me, to take away my reproach."

In the sixth month, the same angel who spoke to Zacharias told Mary of Elisabeth's condition. With great joy, Mary hurried to the hill country of Judea, to the house of Zacharias, to be with her cousin, with whom she shared a most uncommon common bond. Elisabeth, hearing Mary's greeting, felt the babe leap in her womb, and being filled with the Holy Ghost, she exclaimed, "Blessed art thou among women, and blessed is the fruit of thy womb."

These two women—one older and seasoned in life, a rock of faith; the other younger, barely betrothed, beautiful—enjoyed three months of companionship. There must have been joy, laughter, moments solemn and tender, some learning, some growing. In Jerusalem, Roman soldiers marched while the Pharisees busied themselves with ceremonial pieties. The world moved on, thoughtlessly unaware of the domestic drama tucked away in the peaceful hills of Judea.

Shortly after Mary and her cousin separated, Elisabeth gave birth to a son. As had been prophesied, her neighbors and relatives rejoiced with her, gathering on the eighth day to witness the circumcision and naming of the child. How much of the angel's message Zacharias was able to convey to Elisabeth in his incapacitated condition, we do not know—except that she knew her son was to be called John.

The family wanted the child to be named Zacharias as would be proper to honor his father. When Elisabeth insisted on the name of John, the matter was referred to her husband. He wrote with a stylus on a wax tablet, "His name is John." In that instant, the angel's words were fulfilled and Zacharias's tongue was loosened. He praised God.

Those who had come to witness a circumcision now had witnessed the miraculous restoration of Zacharias's speech as well. His sudden affliction in the temple, the birth itself, and now this miracle seemed portentous, to say the least. The people whispered among themselves, "What manner of child shall this be!"

Zacharias, filled with the Holy Ghost, prophesied. He touched on all the predictions of a Messiah from the beginning, concluding with a clear statement of exactly what manner of child this John would be: a prophet; one to go before the Lord, to prepare his ways; one to give knowledge of salvation to the people and light to those who sit in darkness.

The boyhood of John is summarized in a few words: the boy "grew, and waxed strong in spirit, and was in the deserts till the day of his shewing unto Israel." Nothing more is said of Elisabeth. Being older when John was born, it is possible that she died before he began his mission. But her maternal influence is unmistakable.

When Jesus came to be baptized, John greeted his cousin with his mother's very words: "Comest thou to me?" No jealousy, no one-upmanship, no jockeying for position; only love, humility, and an ennobling pride in his own role.

Some time later, when John was questioned by a group of Jews intent on arousing his envy, he stated unequivocally, "I am not the Christ. I am sent before him." Then, calling himself the friend of the bridegroom, the one who has not the bride but rejoices in the bridegroom's voice, he added, "My joy is . . . fulfilled." Now, "he must increase, but I must decrease."

In the same spirit, Jesus honored both Elisabeth and her son when he said, "Among those that are born of women there is not a greater prophet than John the Baptist."

Elisabeth was promised that her son would perform a great mission. To help him, she instilled within him such love and humility that the usual stumbling blocks of hate and envy were swept aside, leaving him free to fulfill his own destiny. What mother could hope to do more?

Scripture references:
*Elisabeth*
Luke 1:5-80; 7:28; Matthew 11:11; John 3:30; Doctrine and Covenants 84:27

# 15

# Mary Magdalene

Mary Magdalene came to the Savior's tomb in the company of other women. Besides herself, there were Mary, the mother of James and Joseph; Joanna; Salome, a woman called simply the mother of Zebedee's children; and perhaps others. Two days earlier they had watched Jesus' hasty burial. In the final hours before the Sabbath, there had been little time to properly prepare the body; Jesus had been quickly wrapped in fresh linen and laid in a new sepulcher. Now, in the earliest dawn of the day following the Sabbath, Mary came with her sisters, bringing spices to more thoroughly anoint and embalm the body, the only loving service left to render the dead.

As they approached the tomb, they expressed concern. Who would roll the large stone from the door? Either as they arrived or shortly before, there was a great earthquake. An angel descended, rolled back the stone, and sat upon it. The keepers Pilate had sent to guard the tomb trembled and "became as dead men." But to the women, the angel said, "Fear not. . . . He is not here; for he is risen."

The angel invited them to see the place, now empty, where the Lord had lain, then commissioned them to go quickly and tell the disciples. Frightened, the women seem only to have understood that Jesus was gone.

Mary hurried to Peter and an unnamed disciple (thought to be John) and said, "They have taken away the Lord out of the sepulchre, and we know not where they have laid him." Peter and John returned with Mary. As she stood outside weeping, they investigated. John peered into the tomb; Peter entered. They saw that the grave was empty; the linen garments that had been wrapped about Jesus were at one end of the place where he had lain. The napkin that was on his head was in a place by itself. Of that moment John wrote, "They knew not the scripture, that he must rise again from the dead." Peter and John left.

Mary lingered. Alone, she entered the tomb. To her eyes it was not empty. She beheld two angels dressed in white, one sitting at the head and the other at the foot of where the body of Jesus had lain.

One of the angels spoke: "Woman, why weepest thou?" It was an odd question given the scene—a sepulcher and a woman bringing spices to anoint the dead. Women had been weeping at the graves of their loved ones since Eve buried her first son. "I will greatly multiply thy sorrow," God had said to Eve. Now, "Woman, why weepest thou?" asked the angel.

But the directness of the question didn't confound Mary. She was not overawed by the vision. With great simplicity, she stated her confusion: "Because they have taken away my Lord, and I know not where they have laid him." Then, becoming aware of someone else standing nearby, and believing it to be the caretaker, she pleaded, "Sir, if thou have borne him hence, tell me where thou hast laid him, and I will take him away."

Jesus spoke her name, "Mary." She turned, instantly recognizing the Master's voice. "Rabboni," she said. So it was that the woman from Magdala, who came seeking the Christ, was found by him. Her own name, "Mary," broke through the darkness of her sorrow and instantly converted her tears to joy. "Mary—Rabboni!"

She fell at his feet, reaching out to embrace him. But she was to learn a second mystery: Jesus must first ascend to the Father. Later, she and many others would touch him, feeling the nail prints and the place where the sword pierced his side. They would sit with him and eat with him, but not yet. First there was a mandate from above to which he must give obedience.

Yet Jesus did not simply leave Mary to ponder the riddle of his new reality. He called her to be a messenger and commissioned her with a specific service: "Go to my brethren, and say unto them, I ascend unto my Father, and your Father; and to my God, and your God."

Mary did not know how the disciples would react to her message. As a matter of fact, she was not well received; they refused to believe that Jesus was alive and that she had seen him.

Shortly after appearing to Mary, Jesus appeared to the other women, saying, "All hail." These women embraced his feet and worshipped him. He charged them also as messengers, saying, "Go tell my brethren." But even when they corroborated Mary's testimony, the disciples only shook their heads and said, "These are the tales of idle women."

Their reaction is not surprising, considering that Mary and her sisters had entered into a new world of understanding. It was an adventure as startling as the one their mother Eve undertook when she sought knowledge like unto God and partook of the forbidden fruit. As the first to behold the risen Christ, the first to witness the miracle with her own eyes and ears, the first to grasp the full significance of the empty tomb, Mary spoke fact in perplexity, giving her witness at the very threshold of the Resurrection.

Who was this Mary Magdalene that she should be honored with the first vision of the risen Christ? The account is brief, but we know that she was an influential woman from the town of Magdala, one of several women who gave her substance as well as her devotion to Jesus' mission. The scriptures tell us that she stood close by the cross when others, even the apostles, tarried afar off. When Jesus asked John to take his mother away, Mary Magdalene remained. The high regard in which the gospel writers held her is evidenced by the fact that she is mentioned by name fourteen times.

Mary seems to have been profoundly grateful to Jesus for having purged her of seven demons. What were those "seven devils"? They could have been evil spirits; or she might have been a victim of epilepsy. Whatever afflicted Mary, Jesus healed her. But Jesus healed many — including the ten lepers, nine of whom didn't even return to thank him. Healing alone did not make converts. Mary's faith must have been based on more than gratitude, for, while there is no account of how she came to the knowledge, she seems to have known exactly who Jesus was. Immediately after her healing, she appears in the scriptures as a fully poised, fully converted woman.

Unfortunately, since medieval times Mary has been much maligned. Her name, "Magdalene," has come to mean "reformed prostitute," and artists have repeatedly depicted her as an immoral woman driven to the Savior by her sins. All this has come about because Bible scholars, beginning in the fourth century, chose to identify her with the unnamed sinful woman of Luke 7:36-50 who washed Jesus' feet with her hair. The first mention of Mary Magdalene in Luke 8:2 follows closely the account of the sinful woman, but there is no reason to assume that the two women are the same. And what is more, the early Christians did not regard Mary as a reformed prostitute. In light of that fact, I think it is safe to assume that Mary Magdalene was never a harlot.

This is not to say that Jesus could not have extended his mercy to a prostitute and converted her into a disciple and close friend. On the other hand, nothing in scripture warrants impugning the chastity of Mary Magdalene.

Because Jesus interacted freely with Mary, Martha, Mary Magdalene, and many other women in a manner that the Jews of his day would have considered improper and highly unbecoming unless he were married, there are those who speculate that Mary Magdalene was his wife. Nothing in scripture refutes that idea, but neither is it supported. In the scriptures she is portrayed as a close friend of the Savior's, a woman of great fortitude. Her love never faltered, and her faith carried her through the dark hours of the Crucifixion. When others fled, she remained. When the two apostles left the tomb, she lingered. Where others' eyes saw emptiness, she saw angels, and it was she who first discerned the risen Christ. Her reward was not only a crown of glory but a closer knowledge of things divine and a sacred commission. She who had been carrying spices to a tomb now threw aside her useless ointments and carried the glorious news: "I have seen the Lord."

Scripture references:
*Mary Magdalene*
Matthew 27:56-61; 28:1; Mark 15:40-47; 16:1-9; Luke 8:2; 24:10; John 19:25; 20:1-18

# 16

# *The Women Who Followed Jesus*

When Mary Magdalene joined the followers of Jesus, she became one of a band of women closely associated with the Savior. The scriptures indicate that these women—Mary Magdalene; Mary, the mother of Christ; Peter's wife; Joanna; Susanna; Salome; Mary, the wife of Cleophas; Mary of Bethany; Martha; Mary, the mother of John Mark; and perhaps others—had access to Jesus. He seems to have sought out and enjoyed their company. They were close friends. He discussed his mission with them, taught them, trusted them, and commissioned them to take his message to others. They, in turn, understood and responded intelligently to his teachings and served vital functions in the work. Many of them ministered to Jesus and supported him with both their services and their means. (See Luke 8:3.)

Other women believers sought out Jesus from time to time during his ministry. With these women, the Savior interacted dynamically. If they needed to be healed, he healed them; if they repented, he forgave them. If they lacked enlightenment, he taught them. Significantly, nearly half of his earthly ministrations dealt primarily with women.

Who were the women closely associated with Jesus? Mary Magdalene and Mary, the mother of Christ, have already been discussed. Peter's wife (sometimes called Simon or Cephas's wife) opened her home to Jesus when he was in Capernaum. He headquartered there and one day healed her mother of a high fever, a miracle included in three of the four gospels. Paul tells us that Peter's wife traveled with Jesus and her husband when they carried the gospel to other parts of Galilee and Judea, as did wives of the other apostles. (See 1 Corinthians 9:5.)

Joanna was the wife of Chuza, the steward of Herod the Tetrarch. She is mentioned as one of several women Jesus healed of sickness or an evil spirit, and she subsequently gave of herself and her means to Jesus and his disciples. She is mentioned as one of the women who, with Mary Magdalene, brought spices to the tomb to embalm the body of Jesus, and she added her testimony to that of Mary Magdalene and the other women who first informed the apostles that Christ had risen. Though the account is brief and incomplete, Joanna appears as a woman of great faith, and the knowledge she gained as she accompanied Jesus and his disciples must have made her a strong member of his missionary group.

Less is known of Susanna. She is mentioned as having been healed by Jesus and as having given freely of her substance to the work. She, too, was one of the first witnesses to see the resurrected Christ.

Salome was the mother of James and John. She was likely prominent in her Galilean community; her husband, Zebedee, had servants who attended to his fishing boats— an indication that he was a man of means. She may also have been a sister to Christ's mother, thus making her Jesus' aunt, although the scriptures are not entirely clear on this point.

Salome is usually remembered as the ambitious mother who, on the Monday before his crucifixion, came to Jesus, worshipped him, and made a special request: Would he seat her two sons to his right and left in his coming kingdom? Such a petition, not surprisingly, caused indignation among the other ten apostles.

Jesus answered, "Ye know not what ye ask." Then, as he frequently did, he used the incident to teach a lesson. Positions of special privilege and prestige were not his to give, but his Father's. Those who wished to be great must be servants, he added, implying that true spiritual greatness was an attribute earned, not given.

Although Salome appeared shameless in her attempt to win favor for her sons, Jesus' rebuke was kindly and spoken with care so as to increase her understanding. She was not the first—nor would she be the last—to confuse worldly position with spiritual greatness. We all come to Christ in different ways, and seeking privilege may have been Salome's way of testifying to her understanding of Jesus' power and purpose, her acknowledgment of his divinity, for she remained faithful to Jesus to the end, never faltering in her service to him or her loyalty to his mission. Such a woman certainly deserves our admiration.

To Salome's credit is the rich spiritual legacy she gave her sons. John the Beloved seemingly comprehended the spirit of Christ's mission the most perfectly of all the apostles. It was John to whom the Savior entrusted the care of his own mother, and to John he granted the privilege of remaining on earth until his second coming. James, also a faithful apostle, became the first of the Twelve to seal his testimony with his blood; his life ended by the sword of Herod Agrippa. In a very real sense, the sons of Salome succeeded in the Lord's work. No matter where they were seated in the Kingdom, she could be proud of them. She was herself an example of unrivaled service.

Mary, the wife of Cleophas, was mother to the apostle James (the lesser, or the younger) and Joseph, both faithful followers of Jesus. Like the other women, she was healed, gave liberal support to Jesus' mission, and carried spices to the tomb. She was among the faithful to whom Jesus appeared, admonishing them to tell the apostles of his Resurrection.

Mary of Bethany and her sister Martha frequently entertained the Savior in their home. It was their brother, Lazarus, whom Jesus raised from the dead. Mary, the mother of John Mark, owned a house in Jerusalem with an upper room where Jesus and the apostles frequently met.

Together these individuals offer a picture of the kind of women Jesus gathered around him. Without exception, all of these women were converted, capable, and deeply aware of the great mission with which they were associated. Their knowledge of things divine may have been faulty at times or incomplete, but they learned and matured under the tutelage of the Savior, their testimonies never wavering.

Jesus acknowledged the faith of women and performed many miracles at their request. He healed Simon's mother-in-law and Jarius's daughter, and he raised the son of the widow of Nain. For his mother, he turned water into wine. The single time he refused such a request was when a Syrophenician woman begged him to heal her daughter of an evil spirit. At first Jesus made no answer at all. When she cried after him, calling him "thou Son of David" (which shows that she recognized him as the Messiah), his disciples asked him to send her away. To them he said, "I am not sent but to the lost sheep of the house of Israel." Still the woman persisted, falling at his feet and pleading, "Lord, help me." Jesus answered, "It is not meet to take the children's bread, and to cast it unto the dogs." Jesus was not insulting this woman. He was referring to the small, much-loved household dogs of the time. But he was testing her faith and perseverance.

The Syrophenician woman fearlessly used his metaphor to express with absolute clarity her convictions: "Yes, Lord:

yet the dogs under the table eat of the children's crumbs."
Jesus was impressed: "O woman, great is thy faith." He
granted her request.

In this and other incidents, Jesus took a personal risk to
help the women who came to him. No class of people were
more denigrated by the Jews than those of pagan birth, such
as the Syrophenician woman, unless it was a woman who
was menstruating or who had just given birth and was still
hemorrhaging. According to Jewish law, such a woman was
"unclean," and any man who touched or was touched by a
woman during her menstrual period must undergo a ritual
cleansing. (See Leviticus 15:27.)

Knowing that, consider the woman who had a
continuous issue of blood. For twelve years she had been an
outcast, considered unclean and unfit to attend religious
services or even to associate in mixed company. Yet somehow she came to believe that if she could but touch the hem
of the Savior's robe, she would be healed. Being unfit to
touch any Jewish male, much less the Messiah, she hoped
not to be noticed as she approached him.

Jesus, walking to the house of Jairus amid a great throng
of people, suddenly turned and asked, "Who touched me?"

Peter expressed the obvious when he replied, "Master,
the multitude throng thee . . . and thou sayest, who touched
me?"

Jesus insisted, "Somebody hath touched me." He added
that he had felt virtue, or healing power, go out of him.

The woman, not able to escape detection, came forward,
knelt, and confessed that she had touched the Savior while in
an unclean condition. At this point the crowd probably
expected Jesus to react in the prescribed manner. But he
didn't wash his clothes, bathe, and segregate himself until
evening. Rather, he praised the woman: "Daughter, be of
good comfort; thy faith hath made thee whole." Remarkable
about the  incident is the fact that the woman was healed the
moment she touched him. Jesus didn't have to risk being
called "unclean" by the Jews in order to help this woman; he
did it to recognize her great faith.

In a similar manner, Jesus risked his good name for the prostitute who washed his feet with her hair. Simon, a Pharisee, in whose house Jesus was being entertained, saw the woman enter with her alabaster box of ointment, weeping, and wash Jesus' feet. Simon said to himself, "This man, if he were a prophet, would have known who and what manner of woman this is that toucheth him."

Jesus, perceiving his thoughts, allowed the woman to anoint his feet while he related the parable of the creditor. One debtor owed him five hundred pence, the other fifty. Neither could pay, so the creditor forgave them both. Then Jesus asked Simon, "Which of them will love him most?"

"He, to whom he forgave most," Simon answered.

Jesus agreed, then pointed out that while Simon had not offered him water to wash his feet, this woman had bathed them with her tears. Only then did he speak directly to the woman, saying, "Thy sins are forgiven. . . . Thy faith hath saved thee."

"Who is this that forgiveth sins?" asked others at the feast. But the newly redeemed woman knew, and rejoiced.

Throughout Jesus' ministry, certain women seem to have understood him while others were blind to his identity and mission. On the American continent, women were among those who heard the voice testifying to his divinity following his crucifixion. Nephite women were among those who felt his pierced side and the prints of the nails in his hands and feet. In Galilee, faithful women ministered to him and were present at the Sermon on the Mount and at the miracle of the loaves and fishes. In Perea, they brought their children to him to be blessed. In Bethany, they sat at his feet and received instruction. Indeed the only redeeming notes in the nightmarish crucifixion episode were the warning of Pilate's wife and the wails of women who mourned for Jesus.

Little is recorded about the wife of Pilate. Historians give us her name, Claudia Procula, and note that she belonged to a distinguished and powerful Roman family. By birth and connection of higher rank than her husband, it was probably her influence at court that gained him his post in Judea. But it was a troubled post, and there is every reason to believe that she was fully aware of the difficult problems of government facing her husband, including the personal danger from Caesar's retribution if rebellion broke out in Jerusalem, That threat in itself would have been sufficient to make her nights sleepless. Yet, at a time when her husband was seemingly following the wisest course by attempting to placate the Jews, she spoke out. She had had a dream—one powerful enough to make her the only human being—male, female, heathen, Jew, or Gentile—to plead for Jesus' release on the day of his trial. "Have thou nothing to do with that just man," she warned her husband.

What she suggested was not politically expedient. Yet she was fearlessly true to whatever light she had—which at best could not have been more than a glimmer of understanding.

There are only thirty-eight words in the book of Matthew about Pilate's wife. But in that brief space, she leaves such an impression on the gospel story that she is known throughout the Christian world. Her few words caused Pilate to hesitate, and he offered Barabbas to the mob. But they only shouted louder to crucify Jesus.

Her action seemed to be the result of two convictions: first, that Jesus was innocent, and second, that her husband would invite disaster if he took action against Jesus. She was right on both counts. Her husband's final acquittal, "I find no fault in this man," confirms the first. The fact that his administration ended abruptly and that he was banished to the south of France, where he reportedly took his own life, confirms the second.

As Jesus walked to his crucifixion, the scriptures tell us that a great company of women wailed and lamented. Jesus was touched by their sympathy, and he who was silent before Herod, before Pilate, and before the mobs screaming for his blood was not silent before them. "Daughters of Jerusalem," he admonished, "weep not for me, but weep for yourselves, and for your children." He was on his way to his final triumph, but Jerusalem would soon be engulfed by a holocaust—a horror many of those weeping women would live to see.

One cannot help drawing a contrast between those weeping women and the lack of faith on the part of the Jews in general. True relationship to Jesus is by the Spirit, not by flesh and blood. Early in his mission, when a woman raised her voice and praised his mother's breasts and womb, Jesus replied, "Rather blessed are they that hear the word of God and keep it." Mary, his mother, did not find perfection in maternity, but in spiritual obedience. And in his dealings with women, Jesus taught repeatedly that there was no superiority in being male or female, Jew or Gentile—only in one's ability to receive nourishment of the Spirit. The women who followed Jesus shared that common characteristic; they were receptive to the Spirit. This was a fact that their Savior acknowledged and honored.

Scripture references:
*Women who followed Jesus*
Luke 8:3; 3 Nephi 17:25
*Peter's wife*
Matthew 8:14-15; Mark 1:30-31; Luke 4:38-39; 1 Corinthians 9:5
*Joanna*
Luke 8:3; 24:10
*Susanna*
Luke 8:2-3
*Salome*
Matthew 20:20-21; 27:56; Mark 16:1-8
*Mary, the wife of Cleophas*
Matthew 27:56-61; 28:1; Mark 15:40-47; 16:1; Luke 24:10; John 19:25
*Syrophenician woman*
Matthew 15:21-28; Mark 7:24-30
*The woman with the twelve-year issue of blood*
Matthew 9:20-22; Mark 5:25-34; Luke 8:43-48 (See Mosaic laws governing menstruation: Leviticus 15:19-33; 18:19; 20:18; see also Ezekiel 22:10; 36:17.)
*Pilate's wife*
Matthew 27:19
*Women weeping at the Crucifixion*
Luke 23:28

# 17

# *Mary and Martha*

T he good servant" is a recurring image in Jesus' teachings. When Salome asked him to favor her two sons
above the other ten apostles, he answered that those
who wished to be great ought to be servants. At the passover
feast, as he broke the bread and blessed the wine, Jesus asked
his apostles whether it were greater to sit at the table or to
wait upon it. They answered that it was greater to sit at the
table. Not necessarily, was the reply; then, referring to himself as the one who served, Jesus admonished his apostles to
follow his example. On yet another occasion, he girded himself with a towel and washed the feet of the apostles over the
objections of Peter. In this manner Jesus fulfilled the
prophecy of Isaiah, who centuries earlier had described the
coming Messiah as a "righteous servant," a "prudent
servant."

Jesus never practiced hierarchy. He related individually to friends, co-workers, harlots, tax collectors, fishermen, rulers of the synagogue—everyone. And he advocated the same behavior from those around him, healing Simon's mother-in-law that she might minister to him, praising the poor in spirit, the meek and the merciful. Yet on one occasion, while visiting in the home of Mary and Martha, he pointedly preferred the less dutiful Mary.

Mary and Martha lived in Bethany, a small village southeast of the Mount of Olives, beside the Jericho Road and not far from the temple at Jerusalem. They were sisters, perhaps widows, living together with their brother Lazarus in comfortable circumstances. They contributed to Jesus' ministry and entertained him often.

The incident for which these two women are best known occurred during the Feast of Tabernacles, a particularly busy time for Jewish women, who had banquets to prepare and arbors of green boughs to construct and decorate in observance of the holidays. Jesus was Mary and Martha's guest, along with many of his close followers and other believers in Bethany.

The scriptures portray an interesting scene. Martha is busy with the preparations, while Mary sits at the Master's feet, listening with great interest to his words. Martha, feeling more and more irritated, at last vents her feelings: "Lord, dost thou not care that my sister hath left me to serve alone?"

We all know that woman. In every language, in every age, Marthas have broken into the discussion with, "How can you sit there doing nothing while I work my fingers to the bone?" In this case, Martha might have left the Savior out of the problem and simply asked Mary to come and help; but she was too angry. She drew Jesus into the argument by implying that he was amiss in allowing Mary to sit at his feet when he could see how hard she was working.

The Savior's reply was remarkably gentle: "Martha, Martha, thou art careful and troubled about many things:

But one thing is needful: and Mary hath chosen that good part, which shall not be taken away from her."

There is no reproof of Martha's desire to provide well; repeating her name implies great kindness. Nor does Jesus sanction neglect on Mary's part. I must believe that she had willingly helped, doing her share and more, before the Master's arrival, or he would not have commended her. But Jesus likely had no desire for a banquet when a simple meal would do. What he wanted was the sisters' receptive attention. He had more to give them than they could give him.

No story in the scriptures speaks more directly to a woman's dilemma than the story of Mary and Martha. Women from the time of birth are trained to "serve" others —parents, children, husbands, even the needy. For many, it has become difficult to approach life from any other perspective. Yet clearly the Savior would not have his servants become distracted with everyday chores when more important things are at stake. The ideals in this story are fundamental to the Christian message—service, yes, but service rooted in spiritual motivation. For service is meaningful only when it is needed, and when we choose to serve, not when it is unnecessary and done out of a slavish sense of duty or by coercion. The Good Servant laid down his life for others; no one took it from him. Our service, if it is to be edifying to ourselves and others, must be of the same tenor.

So, at the Feast of Tabernacles in Bethany that year, Mary chose "the good part." Does that mean she was more devoted to the Savior than was her sister Martha? Unquestionably, the two sisters were of differing temperaments. Martha was the practical, efficient, eagerhearted hostess. Mary was the impulsive, attentive student. Yet they were one in the Spirit, and Jesus understood and loved both of them.

It was to Martha that Jesus first declared, "I am the resurrection, and the life: he that believeth in me, though he were dead, yet shall he live." Mary and Martha's brother Lazarus had been dead four days; he was buried in a tomb. When

Martha heard that Jesus was coming, she ran out to meet him, lamenting "Lord, if thou hadst been here, my brother had not died." How many times had the sisters said that to one another during those four days, struggling to deal with their grief?

But that wasn't all Martha had to say to the Savior. She added, "I know, that even now, whatsoever thou wilt ask of God, God will give it thee." She acknowledged the power of him who stood before her, knowing that Jesus was one with the will of the Father.

Jesus said, "Thy brother shall rise."

Failing to see more than an assurance that her brother would rise with the rest of the dead, Martha replied, "I know that he will rise again in the resurrection."

It was then that Jesus declared himself to be the resurrection and the life, adding "whosoever liveth and believeth in me shall never die. Believest thou this?"

Martha did not have her reawakened brother before her; she saw only Jesus, and he had come too late. Yet she agreed without reservation: "Yea, Lord: I believe that thou are the Christ, the Son of God, which should come into the world."

And where was Mary? She was still in the house mourning. Jesus asked for her, and Martha went to her, saying, "The Master is come, and calleth for thee." Unlike Martha, who went dry-eyed, Mary ran weeping to fall at his feet, echoing her sister's words: "Lord, if thou hadst been here, my brother had not died." Jesus, recognizing the sisters' differing temperaments, asked the weeping Mary, "Where have ye laid him?" And when he was shown, he wept with her. He grieved for a departed friend, for the sorrow of the two sisters, and for the unbelief of many who had come to comfort Mary and Martha.

Jesus' return to Judea at this time was viewed by some of his apostles as dangerous. They had reminded him of the recent attempts on his life and sought to dissuade him. Some even thought their own lives were in danger. Among those at Mary and Martha's house who had come to console the sisters were many prominent people from Jerusalem. A few were impressed by Jesus' concern, saying, "Behold how he loved him!" Others murmured, "Could not this man, which opened the eyes of the blind, have caused that even this man should not have died?" They were similar to and perhaps some of the same who, only days later, were to murmur, "Let him come down from the cross, and we will believe."

Jesus ordered the stone removed. Martha, ever practical, objected, protesting that "by this time he stinketh: for he hath been dead four days."

The Savior quieted her, and the stone was removed. He offered a prayer giving thanks and acknowledging the Father. Then, with a loud voice, Jesus cried for Lazarus to come forth—and he did.

Disbelief does not resist the miracle. If anything, it seeks signs and proofs; but it resists the one who performs the miracle. With their brother restored to them, Mary and Martha now became more believing, more loyal, more devoted than ever, while the jealous-hearted who witnessed the event began immediately to plot against Jesus. The scriptures indicate that from that moment on, they counseled to put him to death.

Six days later, just before the Crucifixion, Jesus and his apostles dined in Bethany. Martha was again in charge of the preparations; Lazarus sat at the table, and many others were present. Mary, impelled to adoration, took a pound of costly ointment, poured it on Jesus' feet, and wiped his feet with her hair, filling the room with fragrance.

Jesus may have told her of his impending death, or she may have inferred it from his remarks. Even so, she did not try to dissuade him from going to Jerusalem. Perhaps she sensed his mission, realizing that some things were worth dying for, and so, following the custom of the time, refreshed and anointed her guest as only kings were honored. This time her sister made no objection, but others, including Judas, did.

Mary spent between sixty and one hundred dollars on

the precious ointment. Judas would accept less than a third of that amount for betraying the Savior. The gift was lavish; yet Jesus accepted it graciously, saying, "Let her alone: against the day of my burying hath she kept this." He further prophesied that the great honor Mary did him would be told wherever his gospel was preached throughout the world. Mary, as well as her gift, had been accepted. And wherever we hear of Mary, we hear of Martha. Their testimonies stand together.

Scripture references:
*Mary and Martha*
Mark 14:3-9; Luke 10:38-42; John 11; 12:1 9

## 18

# *The Woman at the Well and Other Women Jesus Encountered*

J esus treated women with his kindest attention even when they didn't seek him out or were not numbered among his followers. One Sabbath as he passed through a synagogue, he saw a woman bent with an infirmity that for eighteen years had kept her from standing erect. Without waiting for a request from her or a petition from a male member of her family (which would have been proper for the times), he called her to him. Laying his hands upon her, he spoke directly to her, saying, "Thou art loosed from thine infirmity." Immediately she stood erect, glorified God, and gave thanks in a fervent prayer.

Contrast that with the attitude of the priest at the synagogue, who attacked the woman. "There are six days in which men ought to work," he said; "in them therefore come and be healed, and not on the sabbath day"—as if it was her fault that the Savior had noticed and healed her!

Jesus answered the priest as directly as he had addressed the woman: "Thou hypocrite, doth not each one of you on the sabbath loose his ox or his ass from the stall, and lead him away to watering? And ought not this woman, a daughter of Abraham, . . . be loosed from this bond on the sabbath day?"

An animal was a source of income. The woman, in the eyes of the priest, was merely something to be pitied, nothing more. Jesus shamed him with that bare truth.

Jesus engaged women individually, a fact best illustrated by the way he handled an adulterous woman. She was brought to him by a party of Scribes and Pharisees as part of a prearranged attempt by them to find cause against him. The case was not difficult. The woman was guilty; she had been taken in the very act. While it was true that the law of Moses decreed death by stoning for this sin, the practice of such extreme punishment had lapsed, even prior to Roman rule. Yet if Jesus pronounced the old Mosaic law obsolete, the Pharisees could denounce him, and if he admonished them to stone the woman, they could report him for rebellion against Rome. It is obvious that the Pharisees had no concern for the woman, but were preoccupied with their own devices.

Jesus saw the situation differently. It was the Scribes and Pharisees to whom he gave little heed. Stooping down, he traced with his finger on the ground as if he had not heard them. They continued to question him, but when at last he answered, it was with a single terse sentence: "He that is without sin among you, let him first cast a stone at her." Having thus spoken, he went back to writing on the ground. When he looked up again, the Scribes and Pharisees had gone; only the woman remained, still awaiting his decision.

Both Jesus and the woman were aware of her guilt. Nevertheless, he spoke respectfully to her, neither condemning nor condoning. "Where are those thine accusers? hath no man condemned thee?"

"No man, Lord."

"Neither do I condemn thee: go, and sin no more."

Some of the most moving features of Jesus' teachings are reflected in the conversations he had with simple people. The Savior delivered his deepest truths to fishermen, farmers, beggars, and widows, who, for the most part, simply received gratefully what the more learned Scribes and Pharisees wearied with debate. So it was with the Samaritan woman at the well.

Returning to Galilee from Jerusalem, Jesus took the unpopular road through Samaria. Animosity between Jews and the Samaritans dated back to the Exile, when the Israelites who were left behind intermarried with the Assyrian invaders. Half a century later, when those who had been carried to Babylon returned and began to rebuild the temple, they contemptuously refused the help of those Samaritans because they were crossbred. The Samaritans, stung by the rebuff, built their own rival temple on Mount Gerizim, and from that day forth Jews and Samaritans had no dealings with one another. In Jesus' time the Samaritans were known to waylay Jewish pilgrims, while the Jews, regarding Samaritans as Levitically unclean, took elaborate pains to avoid any contact with them. But Jesus crossed Samaria on his way to Galilee, and, coming to the ancient well of Jacob, he rested while his disciples went to purchase food in the nearby village.

A woman came to the well with her pitcher, and Jesus asked a drink of her. She was a woman who had been passed from man to man, which may be the reason she came alone to that well rather than drawing water nearer the village where local women gathered. When Jesus spoke, she was immediately filled with suspicion and inquired, "How is it that thou, being a Jew, askest drink of me, which am a woman of Samaria?" He replied, "If thou knewest . . . who it is that saith to thee, Give me to drink; thou wouldest have asked of him . . . living water."

These were surprising words, but a woman who had held her own with six men was not inclined to be bested in conversation. She retorted, "Thou hast nothing to draw with, and the well is deep: from whence then hast thou that living water?"

Jesus pointed to the well and replied, "Whosoever drinketh of this water shall thirst again: but whosoever drinketh of the water that I shall give him shall never thirst."

The woman, still failing to understand, replied mockingly, "Sir, give me this water, that I thirst not, nor come hither to draw."

Jesus cut her short. "Go, call thy husband, and come hither."

Why that particular command? Was Jesus resorting to proper protocol? He had never resorted to it in the past. Yet it seems unworthy to suppose that he asked solely to embarrass and shame her, knowing what he knew. I prefer to think that he discerned something worthwhile behind the woman's hardened, haughty attitude, and therefore asked the one question sure to open her heart.

"I have no husband," said the woman of Samaria; and, having confessed, she became a different woman, her hardness and raillery gone.

"Thou hast said well," Jesus replied. "For thou hast had five husbands; and he whom thou now hast is not thy husband."

With her past, her innermost heartaches now revealed, what could she answer? "Sir, I perceive that thou art a prophet."

Then, in that marvelous way in which Jesus dealt with the humble and simple in heart, Jesus spoke as freely as water filling a jar. To her question regarding the proper place to worship, he answered, "God is a Spirit: . . . worship him in spirit and in truth."

"I know that Messias cometh, which is called Christ: when he is come, he will tell us all things," she reflected.

"I . . . am he," said Jesus, making the first recorded declaration of his mission.

When Jesus' disciples returned, they marveled that he

was talking with this Samaritan woman. But she had heard enough to be convinced. She ran back to the village and said to the men there, "Come, see a man, which told me all things that ever I did: is not this the Christ?" Perhaps something in the woman's voice, her manner, her eyes, prompted them to listen, and they came from the city to see who it was that knew all.

Jesus and his disciples tarried in the village for two days. At the end of that time, many of the villagers believed—not because of the woman alone but because they had heard for themselves and knew that Jesus was the Christ, the Savior of the world.

Jesus, no respecter of persons, had quickened the spirit of a worldly woman who then drank of his "living water" and was spiritually refreshed. Having partaken, the power she carried with her from the Master's presence was enough to inspire an entire village. Likewise, the adulterous woman and the woman loosed from her eighteen-year infirmity were changed—as is every woman who truly encounters her Savior.

Scripture references:
*Woman healed on sabbath*
Luke 13:11-16
*Adulterous woman*
John 8:3-11; see also Deuteronomy 17:5-6
*Woman at the well*
John 4:7-42

# 19

# *Women of the Early Church*

P erhaps because of our similarity of purpose in spreading the gospel, or because I sense their deep spiritual strength, I feel closer to the women in the early Christian church than to any other of my sisters in the scriptures. Twenty-three individuals, they represent the largest gallery of women named in any period recorded by sacred script. Although many of the references are brief, even cryptic, most of the women emerge as individuals.

What also emerges is the vital role they played in the spread of Christianity. Unquestionably, the early Christian church could not have survived without the nurturance of its female converts, a fact attested to by the homage paid them by the apostles, particularly Peter and Paul. The early Church leaders were indebted to these women for lodging and succor, meetingrooms and places of refuge. When the apostles moved on to carry the gospel to new lands, they charged the women with specific responsibilities to further the work. Women in the early Church filled missions, acted as emissaries, preached, taught, aided the poor, and, in a surprising number of cases, provided the financial where-withal and stability to organize new congregations.

Lydia was such a woman. The first European convert to Christianity, Paul referred to her and other members of the Church in Philippi (nearly all women in the beginning) as his "joy and crown."

Lydia was probably born in the city of Thyatira and later moved to Philippi, an important Macedonian city. There she imported and sold the much-sought-after "purple cloth" for which her native region was famed and from which she took her own name. As a businesswoman, she was a success; more importantly, she was a deeply spiritual person. Business didn't fill her life; the scriptures tell us that she met regularly with a group of women to pray.

Perhaps observations from her business enabled Lydia to distinguish substance from appearance. The "purple" for her cloth was made from the juices of a certain shellfish. While still in the veins of the animal, the juice was white; when removed and exposed to the sun, it took on hues from deepest purple to crimson—a true transformation. But why was the purple-dyed cloth so sought after? Among Lydia's customers were Babylonian merchants who bought it for their temple curtains and for costumes for their idols. Members of the Roman imperial family, pretenders to divinity, wore the cloth on state occasions. Whatever the source of her understanding, Lydia and her prayer group, though small in number, were large in spirit. Undoubtedly it was as a result of their earnest search for the truth that one day Paul and Silas were directed to find them on the banks of a river and preach to them. Their conversion was clearly aided by the Spirit; we are told that the Lord opened Lydia's heart.

Lydia won her whole household to Christianity, and

they were baptized together. Then she "constrained" Paul to stay with her, pleading, "If ye have judged me to be faithful to the Lord, come into my house, and abide there." Her desire to know the gospel was strong at a time when the only way to learn was to sit at the feet of teachers like Paul and Silas, for the gospels had not yet been written. Paul stayed, teaching Lydia and many others in her home. Later Timothy and Luke were her guests, as well as Silas and perhaps others.

Her hospitality drew Paul and Silas to seek refuge in her home after they were delivered from prison—an adventure that draws another contrast between substance and appearance. A young girl who was possessed of a spirit of divination and who had earned her masters a good deal of money by soothsaying began to follow Paul and Silas. For many days she declared them to be servants of the most high God and testified that their message was to show the way to salvation. Paul grieved, for he knew the source of her inspiration. At last he turned and commanded the evil spirit to depart from her. But when her masters saw the means of their income eliminated, they went before the magistrate and had Paul and Silas beaten and cast into prison. At midnight, an earthquake opened the prison doors. After converting the terrified jailer, Paul and Silas came to Lydia, who had also declared them men of God, teachers of the way of salvation. But her knowledge had come from the true Spirit.

Did their adherence to truth make the women of Philippi homogeneous? Hardly. Euodias and Syntyche disagreed with each other. They were sisters in the faith who had labored with Paul; he describes them as having earned places in the Book of Life. Yet their disagreement was serious enough that Paul wrote and admonished them "to be of one mind." He would later give similar counsel to the women of Chloe's household in Corinth when it became the center of religious strife, suggesting that differences were not uncommon among the faithful.

Paul went on to entreat others in Philippi to help with the

reconciliation of Euodias and Syntyche. He added that truth and excellence should be sought wherever such qualities were to be found, suggesting (in words that Joseph Smith paraphrased for the thirteenth Article of Faith) an unlimited spectrum of worthy endeavors, giving the widest possible latitude to individual personalities, talents, and preferences: "Whatsoever things are true, whatsoever things are honest, whatsoever things are just, whatsoever things are pure, whatsoever things are lovely, whatsoever things are of good report; if there be any virtue, and if there be any praise, think on these things. . . . And the God of peace shall be with you."

As in Philippi, a great many remarkable women made up the congregation, and some of the leadership, of the Church in Rome. In his letter to Timothy, Paul sends greetings from Claudia, probably a highly placed Roman matriarch who had joined the Christians. When he wrote to the Church in Rome, he commended Julia as a Saint, Mary for the help she had given him, Tryphena and Tryphosa for their work for the Lord, and Persis, whom he called "beloved." The bearer of his letter was a woman named Phebe, a Christian matron living in the eastern part of Corinth. She was probably a widow, inasmuch as she was able to travel alone and conduct business in her own name. Many, if not most, of the women named in connection with the early Church are thought to have been widows because of the fact that they acted for themselves—a privilege allowed only widows in that day. Many of those upon whom the survival of the early Church depended were likely older women, seasoned in life's school.

Paul must have known Phebe well. In asking her to carry his letter, he conferred a great honor on her. In his letter he introduces her to the Saints in Rome as "our sister," "a servant of the church," "a succorer of many," and, he adds, "of myself also." Likely Paul was as welcome and comfortable in Phebe's home in Cenchrea as he was in Lydia's home in Philippi.

Phebe carried Paul's letter to Rome. Possibly she lost her life there, as did Paul and Apphia, a woman martyr mentioned in a letter Paul wrote from his Roman prison cell to Philemon. Many of the Christians in Rome suffered death at the hands of their persecutors.

Among the Roman persecutors were two sisters, Drusilla and Bernice, whose roles in the affairs of the early Church mark a striking contrast to the faithful. They are mentioned in Acts as being present when Paul appeared in the judgment hall at Caesarea to answer charges of sedition and profanation of the temple, but the main part of their story is found in the writings of Josephus.

They were the daughters of Herod Agrippa I, who attained the distinction of being the first royal persecutor of the Church. They were also great-granddaughters of Herod the Great, who ordered the young male babes of Bethlehem murdered at Christ's birth and caused Mary and Joseph to flee to Egypt with their child. And they were nieces of Herod Antipas, who had John the Baptist beheaded at the request of his wife Herodias and her daughter by another marriage.

Drusilla was married to King Aziz of Emesa, but in defiance of the law she left her husband to marry Felix, procurator of Judea. At the time of Paul's trial she had come to Caesarea to live with Felix. Undoubtedly she knew of Paul; he was famed as the greatest living Christian. When Paul appeared to answer the charges against him, he delivered a memorable discourse touching on righteousness, temperance, and judgment—a sermon that caused her husband to tremble and dismiss the apostle, hoping not to be troubled by him further. Drusilla's reaction to Paul's speech is not recorded, but certainly it differed from that of Lydia or Phebe, for the persecutions continued.

When Paul came a second time to plead his case, Bernice was in attendance. She had been the subject of much gossip because of her incestuous affair with her own brother. Bernice had been married to Herod of Chalcis, but after his death she made no attempt to conceal the fact that she was the official consort of her brother, Agrippa II. She, too, heard a powerful sermon from Paul, at which her brother was heard to remark, "Almost thou persuadest me to be a Christian."

Agrippa II, the Governor, Bernice, and others who heard Paul that day talked among themselves, agreeing that Paul had done nothing worthy of death or prison. Yet they did nothing to release him.

Paul went back to prison to write letters that would reach more people through the ages than would any Roman edict. Bernice, her sister Drusilla, and the rest of their family, whose lives were strangely intertwined with the rise of Christianity, experienced a few worldly pleasures and then disappeared into the obscurity of history.

Being born to a high position is not in itself a spiritual stumbling block, for other women of privilege accepted the Church. When Paul spoke on Mars Hill in Athens, arguing against the Epicureans and Stoics, Damaris listened. Of the Greeks in Thessalonica and Berea, Luke writes that a number of honorable upper-class woman believed. But Damaris is named specifically.

She may have been one of the Hetairai, a group of highly intellectual women in Athens who were associated with philosophers and statesmen, for few others of her sex would have enjoyed the freedom to act as she did.

But more important than her class or education was her spiritual receptiveness. When Paul preached that the God who made the world and everything in it did not live in a shrine, some mocked; others, feeling no urgency, said they would consider the matter. Damaris and two men, Dionysius and Areopagite, believed and clung to him as he departed.

The Candace of Ethiopia ("candace" meaning "queen") may also have been receptive to Christianity. She is mentioned in connection with the eunuch in charge of her treasury, who traveled to Jerusalem to worship. There he met Phillip, who expounded the scriptures for him. He

believed Jesus Christ to be the Son of God and asked to be
baptized. After baptizing him, Phillip was caught away by
the Spirit; the eunuch saw him no more but went on his way
rejoicing. The Candace of Ethiopia must have been partial to
the eunuch or she would not have allowed him to travel such
a distance to worship; it is likely that he reported his conversion to her. Whether she believed or not, she would have
been one of the first in the high circles of Ethiopia to hear the
message of Jesus Christ.

Other women not only heard but spread the gospel
message. One who was particularly active as a teacher and
missionary was Priscilla. Leaving Rome with her husband
Aquila at the time when Claudius expelled all Jews, she
traveled first to Corinth, then to Ephesus. The couple were
tentmakers. Paul, also a tentmaker by trade, lived and
worked with them in Corinth, going to the synagogue on the
Sabbath to persuade the Jews and the Greeks. It is known
that the Church members assembled in Priscilla's home in
Rome and later in Ephesus. In Corinth, her home, located in
the weaving section of the city, was a rendezvous for those
wanting to know more about the new faith.

When Paul left Corinth, he took Priscilla and Aquila
with him to Ephesus, where Paul credits them with saving
his life during the anti-Christian riots. Forced to leave, he
committed the work to their supervision, returning more
than a year later to find an organized functioning congregation. Some time later, after the death of Claudius ended the
worst of the persecutions, Priscilla and her husband returned
to Rome.

Priscilla was probably one of the most influential women
in the early Church. Unquestionably, she was known
throughout the Christian world of her day and was close
enough to Paul that he referred to her using the familiar
diminutive of her name, "Prisca." Though she and her
husband labored together, in three out of five instances
where their names appear, hers is mentioned first—an
unprecedented breaking of convention, leading many Bible

scholars to believe that she played the more important role.

Priscilla is best known as the teacher of the eloquent and learned Apollos, a Jew from Alexandria who had first learned of the gospel from John the Baptist but whose understanding was incomplete. Although Apollos taught baptism by immersion, he did not understand the significance of the death and resurrection of Jesus Christ. Nevertheless, he had earned a name for himself as a persuasive speaker for the new faith. His popularity at times rivaled Paul's. Realizing the damage that someone of his talents might do to the true Christian cause, Priscilla undertook to teach him the ways of God more perfectly. No superficial convert herself, she invited Apollos into her home and expounded the scriptures to him. She must have been a woman of some scholarly attainments, for Apollos is described as being "mighty in the scripture." Still, she prevailed, and Apollos became a truly great missionary for the Church.

Priscilla's fame is of such magnitude that she is mentioned in records other than the Bible. She is probably the best known of all the women named in Acts or in the epistles. She managed a household, worked at her trade, studied the gospel (probably as Paul's most competent and inspired pupil), preached with her husband, taught, fellowshipped, and, though no mention is made of children, probably reared a family. She juggled the same demands as those placed on women in the Church today, and she managed well enough that her home, no matter where it happened to be—Rome, Corinth, or Ephesus—was always open to Paul and the other brethren.

Yet no home was better known or more consecrated than that of Mary, the mother of John (surnamed Mark). Hers was the house in Jerusalem with an upper room where Jesus and his followers often met, and which remained a meeting-place for the early Christians as long as she lived. It was here that the Pentecost took place, when the Holy Spirit descended upon the apostles and they spoke in tongues, prophesied, and were imbued with the desire to go to all the world with the Master's message.

It was to Mary's home that Peter came directly from prison. Mary's maid, Rhoda, was keeping guard at the door of the upper room while a group of the disciples prayed for Peter. A knock came.

"Who is it?" she asked, perhaps fearing that members of the Sanhedrin had come to trap the Christians.

"Peter," was the answer.

She knew his voice and ran to tell the others. They refused to believe her until they came to the door themselves, let Peter in, and heard him tell of his miraculous deliverance.

Mary and her servant Rhoda were fortunate, for they knew Jesus personally. Most of the other women who embraced the early Church belonged to that group Jesus described as "blessed, [for they] have not seen, and yet have believed." (See John 20:29.) The witness of truth, whether it comes from personal knowledge or by the Spirit, is such an individual, personal experience that it is natural to wonder and rejoice in the discovery that the same testimony burns within the heart of a loved one. Mary was fortunate in this regard, too; her son John Mark wrote one of the gospels (Mark). He was the friend and companion that Peter referred to as "Marcus my son." He, along with Barnabas, Mary's close relative, perhaps her nephew, accompanied Paul on his first mission.

Mothers in the early Church, like mothers today, prepared their sons for missions. Paul credits Eunice and Lois for the fine upbringing of Timothy: "The . . . faith that is in thee . . . dwelt first in thy grandmother Lois, and thy mother Eunice," he wrote. Paul converted Timothy on his first missionary journey; Timothy then accompanied Paul on his second mission, becoming like a son to him. Though nothing more is said of his mother and grandmother, that one reference is reason enough to honor them as worthy women.

One cannot feign faith and still hope to receive its rewards. Yet Sapphira tried to do just that; she wanted credit for having given all to the Church without actually doing so.

Sapphira and her husband Ananias were among the wealthier Christians. They joined the Saints at a time when outpourings of the Holy Ghost were particularly strong; they witnessed miracles, the gift of tongues, and other manifestations. Undoubtedly, they were aware that Barnabas had sold all his goods and given the money to the Church. Indeed, the common order among Christians in Jerusalem was so successful that there were no needy among them. Yet there was no coercion to join the common community; it was not required. Nevertheless, Ananias and Sapphira agreed voluntarily to share all they had. Their pledge, though sacred, could have been withdrawn; even after they sold their land, the proceeds belonged to them, to keep or share as they chose. In the end, Ananias and Sapphira conspired to hold back a part of their money but pretended to give all. First Ananias and later Sapphira lied to Peter, making a hypocrisy of their generosity. For their deception they were both instantly struck dead. A harsh punishment? Perhaps, if the sin had been holding back money. But their sin lay in bearing false witness when they had knowledge of the Holy Ghost—more knowledge than most.

Dorcas, on the other hand, regained her life because of her generosity. She lived in Joppa, a port city thirty-four miles northwest of Jerusalem, in what became an important Christian center. Her home, like those of many of her sisters, became a gathering spot for those of the new faith. More than that, it was a place of refuge and help for the poor. Dorcas, a woman of means, could have given the poor money and sent them on their way, but she chose to give of her time and her service as well. She sewed for those who needed clothes.

There are always the poor—and never an end to hardship and misfortune. Dorcas may have had moments when she grew weary, despaired, or thought her example had little impact. But when she died, it was the widows and orphans she had helped who sent for Peter.

The apostle was preaching in a nearby town. He came at

once, and when he entered the room where Dorcas lay, the widows who wept there showed him the coats and garments she had sewn for them. They might have wished to impress Peter with the goodness of this woman, or perhaps they feared what would become of them with their benefactor gone. Peter cleared the room, knelt, and prayed. Using the Aramaic form of her name, Tabitha, he called Dorcas, and she arose from the dead. Giving her his hand, he lifted her up and presented her to the widows—alive. The miracle became known throughout all Joppa. Because of it, we are told, many believed.

Nothing more is recorded of Dorcas. She probably continued serving, "full of good works and almsdeeds," with renewed vigor and purpose. All of the accounts of women in the early Church are sketchy, barely highlighting the essentials of their faith and good works. Yet we can be impressed with the number of women who won recognition from the writers of scripture.

We can be even more impressed at the way they stand out as real women, doing real things for real reasons. These are not idealized, superficial women filling stylized roles as outlined for them by the customs of their times. These are women we can learn from and emulate, for the world will always have need of more Dorcases and Lydias, Phebes and Priscillas.

Scripture references:
*Lydia*
Acts 16:14-40
*Eurodias and Syntyche*
Phillippians 4:2-9
*Chloe*
1 Corinthians 1:11
*Roman women*
Romans 16:6-15; 2 Timothy 4:21; Philemon 1:2
*Phebe*
Romans (entire epistle, but especially 16:1-2)
*Drusilla and Bernice*
Acts 24:24-25; 25:13-24; 26:18-31

*Damaris*
Acts 17
*Candace of Ethiopia*
Acts 8:27-39
*Priscilla*
Acts 18:2-28; Romans 16:3-5; 1 Corinthians 16:19; 2 Timothy 4:19
*Mary, the mother of John Mark*
Acts 12:12-13; Romans 16:6; 1 Peter 5:13; Acts 1:13; 2:1
*Rhoda*
Acts 12:12-17
*Eunice and Lois*
2 Timothy 1:5-7
*Sapphira*
Acts 5:1-11; see also Acts 2:44-45; 4:32-37
Dorcas
*Acts 9:36-42*

# Index